First World War
and Army of Occupation
War Diary
France, Belgium and Germany

42 DIVISION
Divisional Troops
429 Field Company Royal Engineers
1 March 1917 - 29 March 1919

WO95/2650/3

The Naval & Military Press Ltd
www.nmarchive.com
Published in association with The National Archives

Published by

The Naval & Military Press Ltd

Unit 10 Ridgewood Industrial Park,

Uckfield, East Sussex,

TN22 5QE England

Tel: +44 (0) 1825 749494

www.naval-military-press.com

www.nmarchive.com

This diary has been reprinted in facsimile from the original. Any imperfections are inevitably reproduced and the quality may fall short of modern type and cartographic standards.

© **Crown Copyright**
Images reproduced by permission of The National Archives, London, England, 2015.

Contents

Document type	Place/Title	Date From	Date To
Heading	WO95/2650/3		
Heading	42nd Division 429th Field Coy R.E. Mar 1917-Mar 1919		
Heading	War Diary Of 429 (E.L.) Fld. Coy R.E. From 1st To 31st March. 1917 (Volume 4)		
War Diary	Alexandria	01/03/1917	12/03/1917
War Diary	Marseilles	12/03/1917	13/03/1917
War Diary	Pont Remy	14/03/1917	14/03/1917
War Diary	Hocquincourt	14/03/1917	27/03/1917
War Diary	Merelessart	27/03/1917	29/03/1917
War Diary	Chuignes	29/03/1917	29/03/1917
War Diary	Chuignolles	30/03/1917	31/03/1917
Heading	429 Field Co R.E. (T). 1st to 30th April 1917 (Volume 4)		
War Diary	Chuignolles	01/04/1917	08/04/1917
War Diary	Peronne	08/04/1917	30/04/1917
Heading	429th Field Coy R.E. T. E. May 1917 Volume 2		
War Diary	Peronne	01/05/1917	01/05/1917
War Diary	Epehy	01/05/1917	18/05/1917
War Diary	Villers-Faucon	19/05/1917	20/05/1917
War Diary	Fins	20/05/1917	22/05/1917
War Diary	Dessart Wood	22/05/1917	27/05/1917
War Diary	Bus	27/05/1917	31/05/1917
Heading	War Diary Of 429 Field Co R.E. T. F. From 1st To 30th June 1917 Volume 3		
War Diary	Bus Map France 1/40000 0246	01/06/1917	03/06/1917
War Diary	Havrincourt Wood P18 Central	04/06/1917	07/06/1917
War Diary	Havrincourt Wood Map 57c P18 Cent	08/06/1917	15/06/1917
War Diary	Havrincourt Wood 57c P 18 Cent	17/06/1917	30/06/1917
Heading	War Diary 429 Field Co R.E. From 1st To 31st July 1917 Volume 3		
War Diary	Havrincourt Wood	01/07/1917	07/07/1917
War Diary	Ytres	08/07/1917	08/07/1917
War Diary	Barastre	08/07/1917	09/07/1917
War Diary	Achiet-Le-Petit	09/07/1917	31/07/1917
Heading	War Diary 429 Field Coy R.E. August 1917 Volume 3		
War Diary	Achiet Le Petit	01/08/1917	21/08/1917
War Diary	Bouzincourt Near Albert	21/08/1917	23/08/1917
War Diary	Poperinghe Belgium	23/08/1917	29/08/1917
War Diary	Vlamertinghe	29/08/1917	31/08/1917
War Diary	Ypres	31/08/1917	31/08/1917
Heading	War Diary 429 Field Coy R.E. September 1917 Volume 3		
War Diary	Ypres	01/09/1917	16/09/1917
War Diary	Re Park Brandhoek	16/09/1917	17/09/1917
War Diary	Busseboom	17/09/1917	19/09/1917
War Diary	Poperinghe	19/09/1917	20/09/1917
War Diary	Winnezeele Area	20/09/1917	22/09/1917
War Diary	Coxyde	22/09/1917	23/09/1917
War Diary	Nieuport Bains	24/09/1917	30/09/1917

Heading	429 Field Coy R.E. October 1917 Volume 3.		
War Diary	Nieuport Bains	01/10/1917	06/10/1917
War Diary	Nieuport	06/10/1917	31/10/1917
Heading	429 Field Co Royal Engineers November 1917 Volume 3		
War Diary	Nieuport	01/11/1917	19/11/1917
War Diary	Coxyde	19/11/1917	19/11/1917
War Diary	Uxem	19/11/1917	19/11/1917
War Diary	Teteghem	20/11/1917	20/11/1917
War Diary	Wylder Wormouldt Area	20/11/1917	21/11/1917
War Diary	Zermezeele (Wormouldt Area)	21/11/1917	22/11/1917
War Diary	Le Nieppe (Staple Area)	22/11/1917	23/11/1917
War Diary	La Roupie (Mr Aire)	24/11/1917	25/11/1917
War Diary	La Roupie	26/11/1917	26/11/1917
War Diary	Mt Bernenchon	26/11/1917	27/11/1917
War Diary	Gorre	27/11/1917	30/11/1917
Heading	429 Field Coy R.E. December 1917 Volume 3		
War Diary	Gorre	01/12/1917	04/12/1917
War Diary	Gorre	01/12/1917	31/12/1917
Heading	429th Field Coy Royal Engineers January 1918 Volume 4		
War Diary	Gorre	01/01/1918	05/01/1918
War Diary	Gorre	01/01/1918	31/01/1918
War Diary	Courses	06/01/1918	26/01/1918
War Diary	Gorre	26/01/1918	31/01/1918
Diagram etc	Baby Elephant Shelters		
Heading	429th Field Co R.E. February 1918 Volume 4		
War Diary	Gorre	01/02/1918	13/02/1918
War Diary	Les Harisoirs Commune de Mont Bernenchon Near St Venant	13/02/1918	19/02/1918
War Diary	Les Harisoirs	15/02/1918	20/02/1918
War Diary	Hinges	20/02/1918	28/02/1918
War Diary	Les Harisoirs	16/02/1918	19/02/1918
War Diary	Hinges	21/02/1918	21/02/1918
War Diary	Gorre	01/02/1918	01/02/1918
War Diary	Hinges	24/02/1918	24/02/1918
War Diary	Hinges	20/02/1918	20/02/1918
War Diary	Les Harisoirs	17/02/1918	17/02/1918
War Diary	Hinges	28/02/1918	28/02/1918
Miscellaneous	Narrative Of Raid Carried Out By 1/9th Manchesters And Party Of 429 Field Coy RE	08/02/1918	08/02/1918
Miscellaneous	Copy Of Addendum No 2 To 126th Infty Bde Order No 84	11/02/1918	11/02/1918
Miscellaneous	Memo Ref Strength Equipment And Work Of R E Party Engaged In Raid		
Heading	42nd Divisional Engineers 429th Field Company R.E. March 1918		
Heading	429th Field Coy R.E. March 1918 Volume 4		
War Diary	Hinges	01/03/1918	14/03/1918
War Diary	Oblinghem	14/03/1918	23/03/1918
War Diary	Adinfer Ayette Ayette	23/03/1918	24/03/1918
War Diary	Log East	24/03/1918	24/03/1918
War Diary	Achiet-Le-Grand	25/03/1918	25/03/1918
War Diary	A28B02 (57CNW 1/20000)	25/03/1918	25/03/1918
War Diary	A28B02 Lofeast Wood	25/03/1918	25/03/1918
War Diary	Logeast Wood	25/03/1918	26/03/1918

Type	Location	Start	End
War Diary	Logeast Wood Essarts	26/03/1918	26/03/1918
War Diary	Essarts	27/03/1918	27/03/1918
War Diary	Essarts F19C 57D NE	27/03/1918	27/03/1918
War Diary	Essarts	28/03/1918	29/03/1918
War Diary	Gommecourt	30/03/1918	31/03/1918
War Diary	Essarts	31/03/1918	31/03/1918
Heading	429th Field Company R.E. April 1918		
Heading	429th Field Co R.E. April 1918 Volume 4		
War Diary	E23c64 (57Dne 1/20000)	01/04/1918	02/04/1918
War Diary	F22 Central	02/04/1918	03/04/1918
War Diary	E23c64	04/04/1918	08/04/1918
War Diary	Henu	09/04/1918	16/04/1918
War Diary	Sailly-au-Bois	16/04/1918	25/04/1918
War Diary	Coigneux J3 b 5.6	26/04/1918	30/04/1918
Heading	429th Field Co R.E. May 1918 Volume 4		
War Diary	Coigneux J3 B 5.6	01/05/1918	06/05/1918
War Diary	Covin J.1.b8.4.	07/05/1918	31/05/1918
War Diary	Courses Etc	08/05/1918	26/05/1918
Heading	429th Field Co R.E. June 1918 Volume 4		
War Diary	Covin	01/06/1918	01/06/1918
War Diary	J1b 8.4	02/06/1918	06/06/1918
War Diary	Covin	07/06/1918	07/06/1918
War Diary	W. of Sailly (J17c 1.2)	08/06/1918	30/06/1918
Heading	429th Field Coy RE July 1918 Volume 4		
War Diary	W. of Sailly-au-Bois J 17c 1.2	01/07/1918	05/07/1918
War Diary	W. of Sailly-au Bois	06/07/1918	31/07/1918
War Diary	W. of Sailly-au-Bois J17c 1.2	04/07/1918	31/07/1918
Heading	429th Field Coy RE August 1918 Volume 4		
War Diary	Sailly	01/08/1918	24/08/1918
War Diary	Luke Copse	24/08/1918	25/08/1918
War Diary	Miraumont	26/08/1918	28/08/1918
War Diary	Pys M2d7.6	29/08/1918	29/08/1918
War Diary	Lebaryue M 11b7.5	30/08/1918	30/08/1918
War Diary	Lebaryue	30/08/1918	31/08/1918
Heading	429th Field Coy RE September 1918 Volume 4		
War Diary	Le Barque	01/09/1918	03/09/1918
War Diary	Barastre	04/09/1918	05/09/1918
War Diary	Pys	06/09/1918	21/09/1918
War Diary	Pys And Le Bus Quiere	22/09/1918	22/09/1918
War Diary	Le Bus Quiere	23/09/1918	28/09/1918
War Diary	Bertincourt	29/09/1918	30/09/1918
Heading	429th Field Coy. R.E. October 1918 Volume 4		
War Diary	Bertincourt	01/10/1918	01/10/1918
War Diary	Trescault	02/10/1918	09/10/1918
War Diary	Lesdains	10/10/1918	11/10/1918
War Diary	Beauvois	12/10/1918	23/10/1918
War Diary	Solesmes	24/10/1918	31/10/1918
Heading	War Diary November 1918 Volume 4 429th Field Coy RE		
War Diary	Solesmes	01/11/1918	04/11/1918
War Diary	Le Quesnoy	05/11/1918	05/11/1918
War Diary	Le Carnoy	06/11/1918	07/11/1918
War Diary	Petit Bayay	07/11/1918	08/11/1918
War Diary	Petit Bayay & Boussieres	09/11/1918	09/11/1918
War Diary	Louvroil	10/11/1918	10/11/1918
War Diary	Louvroil & Perriere	11/11/1918	12/11/1918

War Diary	Louvroil Ferriere Hautmont	13/11/1918	13/11/1918
War Diary	Hautmont An Ferriere	14/11/1918	16/11/1918
War Diary	Hautmont	17/11/1918	30/11/1918
Heading	429th Field Coy R.E. December 1918 Volume 4		
War Diary	Hautmont	01/12/1918	06/12/1918
War Diary	Hautmont Vieux Reng And Charleroi	07/12/1918	15/12/1918
War Diary	Charleroi	16/12/1918	31/01/1919
Heading	429th Field Coy R E. February 1919 Volume 5		
War Diary	Charleroi	01/02/1919	28/02/1919
Heading	429th Field Co. R.E. March 1919 Volume 5		
War Diary	Charleroi Belgium	01/03/1919	29/03/1919

WO 95
2650/3

42ND DIVISION

429TH FIELD COY R.E.

MAR 1917 - MAR 1919

Vol. 2

CONFIDENTIAL.

War Diary
of
429 (E.L.) Fd. Coy. R.E.

from 1st to 31st March. 1917

(Volume 4)

Army Form C. 2118.

WAR DIARY
—or—
INTELLIGENCE SUMMARY
(Erase heading not required.)

Instructions regarding War Diaries and Intelligence Summaries are contained in F. S. Regs., Part II. and the Staff Manual respectively. Title pages will be prepared in manuscript.

Place	Date	Hour	Summary of Events and Information	Remarks and references to Appendices
Ottawa	March 1914		Packing up stores prior to embarkation	
ALEXANDRIA	2		Loading Patron waggons etc on board ship	
	3	0930	Major AN LAWFORD, Capt FE BUTTON, 2/Lt KENDALL and 153 O.R. embarked H.T. MENOMINEE	
	AH.12		Voyage, good weather. Stood to the station 2130 March 11th	
MARSEILLES	12	0900	Disembarked	
	12	1300	Entrained	
	13		Train journey	
PONT-REMY	14	1400	Detrained & marched to HOCQUINCOURT	
HOCQUINCOURT	14	1800	Arrived, billetted Company	
do	15		2/Lt STONER & BATEMAN with 20 O.R. reported unit. Took over billets at HALLENCOURT	
do	16 + 17		⇃ O ISEMENT	
do			General RE work for 127 Bde.	
do	18		Lt Col AN LAWFORD & 40 R proceeded to 1st Division for instruction. 9 NCos proceeded to FLIXICOURT for course in rapid wiring. 2/Lt KENDALL 744 Section to FLIXICOURT to duty with 4th Army infantry school. Practice drill for rest of Company	
do	19		Wiring practice, lectures, entrenchments exercises by transport	

429 FF GRE

WAR DIARY
or
INTELLIGENCE SUMMARY.
(Erase heading not required.)

Army Form C. 2118.

Place	Date	Hour	Summary of Events and Information	Remarks and references to Appendices
HICQUINCOURT	20 and 20		bomb practice, Coy drill, gas lectures	ohill
do	21			ohill
do	22		9 NCOs returned from survey course	ohill
do	23		2/Lt AM LAMFORD & 40 R returned from 1st Division Coy on tramway work	ohill
do	24		Coy Training	ohill
do	25			ohill
do	26		Capt BUTTON, 2/Lt SINCLAIR & BATEMAN & 102 OR to ERINDELLE for bridging practice	ohill
			HQ Coy & No3 section to MERELESSART.	ohill
HICQUINCOURT	27	0900		ohill
MERELESSART	27	1000	arrived	ohill
do	28			ohill
do	29	0430	Left & entrained at Pont REMY for CHUIGNES	ohill
CHUIGNES	29	1330	arrived marched to CHUIGNOLLES	ohill
CHUIGNOLLES	30		bombing, lathe, wiring, Coy training	ohill
do	31	0900	2/Lt SINCLAIR & BATEMAN with Nos 1 & 2 Section left for HERBERCOURT.	ohill

Col M Murphy OC
429 Coy RE

WAR DIARY
or
INTELLIGENCE SUMMARY.
(Erase heading not required.)

Army Form C. 2118.

Vol 3

429 FIELD Co. R.E. (T.)

1st to 30th APRIL 1917.

(VOLUME 4)

WAR DIARY
or
INTELLIGENCE SUMMARY
(Erase heading not required.)

Army Form C. 2118.

Instructions regarding War Diaries and Intelligence Summaries are contained in F.S. Regs., Part II. and the Staff Manual respectively. Title pages will be prepared in manuscript.

Place	Date	Hour	Summary of Events and Information	Remarks and references to Appendices
CHUIGNOLLES	April 1	0900	Strength of Coy 2 offs 204 OR 1 officer 26 OR of 5 Manchester attached. 8 OR of 1/27 Bn attached for Bn workshop.	O/M
		1500	1 officer 26 OR from each of B 7-8 = 8 = 9 Manchester reported for pioneer attached duties. Training rapid wiring, pontoon drill	O/M
	2		Training pioneers carrying out Diamond R.E. work	O/M
	3		15 Jrs from HERBECOURT to 42 Div HQ MERICOURT to work on DHQ. 16 other ranks to HERBECOURT to replace above men. Coy had Bde Inspection fitted.	O/M
	4		Wnt to DHQ. Training infantry in rapid wiring. Fitting water carts with pumps for pet. tin distn	O/M
5/6/11		ditto		O/M
	7		" " In 4 Section arrived from FLIXECOURT	O/M
	8	0930	Coy moved less 2/Lt STONER + 35 OR left for Peronne.	O/M
PERONNE	8	1600	Arrived billeted in FAUBERG DE PARIS. Refauns hole in BOULEVARD ROAD all may St	O/M
	9		On BOULEVARD ROAD all day. G.E. visited work in afternoon. No 2 Section in HERBECOURT - Blacketend. No 1 Section in PERONNE - BUSSU - DOINGT roads, working parties for repair of above and supplies from 21st 12th & 48th divisions.	O/M
	10		Road repairing by all the Company. Commenced work on BOULEVARD ROAD break in girder.	O/M

U29 Co

WAR DIARY
or
INTELLIGENCE SUMMARY.
(Erase heading not required.)

Army Form C. 2118.

Place	Date	Hour	Summary of Events and Information	Remarks and references to Appendices
PERONNE	April 11		Road repairs in and around PERONNE	O/WD
	12.13.14.		ditto	O/WD
	15		2/Lt Johnson stopped Coy. Roads Officer returned. Road repairs. Sign writing.	O/WD
	16		Capt BUTTON proceeded on leave. Road repairs. Repairs to PERONNE station yard. General work &c.	O/WD
			C.S.M. Carroll injured & removed to Hospital. 2/Lt BATEMAN acting adjutant	O/WD
	17		Street train arrived at PERONNE. Road repairs. Repairs to PERONNE station. Making signs traction.	O/WD
	18		Started fittings up Divisional Baths, hospital for A.D.M.S. Road repairs.	O/WD
	19.20		ditto	O/WD
	21		ditto	O/WD
PERONNE	21	1600	Moved billets to GRAND PLACE PERONNE	O/WD
	22		Unloading store trains, road repairs. 2/wounded billets hospital being fitted	O/WD
	23.24		ditto	O/WD
	25		Section 1/427 Q.E. taken to BUSSU - Sy DST - TINCOURT road (Mef 62c) Road repair & ammunition H	O/WD
	26		Return of reinforcement camp. 2/Lt R.G. SHARP arrived for duty with Coy. Road repairs. Reporting traces to DADS	O/WD
	27		Capt BUTTON from leave. Work on fr 26th	O/WD
	28.		Work for fr 26. 7 o.r.'s Marched Power from detachment at BUSSU	O/WD

A.M. Murphy H/Lt
4/9 C.R.E.

WAR DIARY
or
INTELLIGENCE SUMMARY.
(Erase heading not required.)

Army Form C. 2118.

Place	Date	Hour	Summary of Events and Information	Remarks and references to Appendices
PERONNE	29.		Work as of preceding days.	O/M
	30	11.53a	Orders received to move to ETINEHY at 5.0pm May 1st	O/M
	30		Work as of preceding day. An infantry working party.	O/M
			Strength 6 Officers 198 O.R. includes balance	O/M
			Attached 4 Officers 112 O.R. Pioneers	O/M
			1 Officer 30 O.R. for work under Ent. Roads Officer	O/M
			— 11 O.R. from 427 GHQ	O/M
			— 1 O.R. from 428 for work under C.R.O.	O/M
			11 325	

O.M.Naylor(?)
429 GRE

Army Form C. 2118.

WAR DIARY
or
INTELLIGENCE SUMMARY.
(Erase heading not required.)

429th FIELD Coy. R.E. T.F.

MAY. 1917.

VOLUME 2

Vol 4

WAR DIARY or INTELLIGENCE SUMMARY

Army Form C. 2118.

(Erase heading not required.)

Place	Date 1917	Hour	Summary of Events and Information	Remarks and references to Appendices
PERONNE	May 1		Strength of Coy. 4 officers 196 other ranks (incl. 6 Bombers) (incl. 1 officer attached HQ RE) 4 " 112 " Infantry Brigade attached Attached officer 2 " 3 " for works under Corps Roads Officer. a 3.8 Other Ranks 1 " 11 " Transport R.E. " From 429 Field Coy. R.E.	
			Total 12 — 325	
		05.00	Lt.Col. A.N. HAWFORD, Capt F.E. BUTTON, 2 Lt STONER & SHARP left with Company & two 2 Lts KENDALL, Lt JOHNSON (roads officer) & Lt LEIGHTON 2nd Lt SINCLAIR left for EPEHY yesterday as advance officer. Arrived.	
"	" 2		Works last night. Redoubts on Brown line, redoubts "L" & "M" returned at PERONNE handed over to Lt BARRETT, 475 Field Coy. RE all wire in hand. Billets stables &c.	WB
EPEHY	" 3		Worked last night on dugouts, kept also wiring.	WB
"	" 4	12.00	Advance party to PERONNE arrived. Captain BUTTON to hospital. Company working parties off 127 Infy. Bde. working nightly on wiring & entrenchments in the Green line, on the left sub-sector. The BLUE LINE is in advance of the GREEN LINE which forms the outpost line at present. The BROWN LINE is at present the main line of resistance but on after the 6th inst. the GREEN LINE becomes the main line of resistance. This is the most northerly sector of the line under the command of the III Corps, another Bde of the 42 Div is on the right. I with	WB WB

Army Form C. 2118.

WAR DIARY
or
INTELLIGENCE SUMMARY.
(Erase heading not required.)

Instructions regarding War Diaries and Intelligence Summaries are contained in F.S. Regs., Part II. and the Staff Manual respectively. Title pages will be prepared in manuscript.

Place	Date	Hour	Summary of Events and Information	Remarks and references to Appendices
EPEHY	May 4		With the 59th DIV. on the right of the 8th DIV. XV Corps. On the left of this sector is the 42 DIV.	
			WIRING. The old German wiring at 40/50 yds in front of the GREEN LINE stands and a double apron fence is being put round each strong point, of which there are 12 in the left end sector, namely "L", "M". The strong points to be wired up also.	
	5		Work last night on previously wired front to enemy reinforcement	
	6		do Col LANFORD attached Engineer F.S.H. NICOLSON reported to enemy reinforcement	
			at 127 Bde HQrs today.	
	7		Work last night is permanently wiring now completed. Finishing of connecting up trench batteries strong points. Making out Communication trenches.	
	8	10.00	H. SHARP left to 4th Army School of Instruction FINSCOURT. Work last night for M.G. emplts — also Communication trenches. Covered 127 Bde. He proposed work in Communication trench	
	9		Last night:- digging Communication trenches, strengthening wiring rearranging safe in old German went. Improvement of trenches strong points	
	10		Last night — Work on forward right. C.O went round right Emb. sup. left sect with Major CLISSOLD to 4th BUCKETT took new right outside left actn from 474 Field Co — to KENDALL	
	11	11.00		
		6pm	wiring round with Lt WILSON (Petrol)	

A.834 Wt. W4973/M687 750,000 8/16 D.D. & L. Ltd. Forms/C.2118/13

WAR DIARY or INTELLIGENCE SUMMARY.

Army Form C. 2118.

(Erase heading not required.)

Instructions regarding War Diaries and Intelligence Summaries are contained in F. S. Regs., Part II. and the Staff Manual respectively. Title pages will be prepared in manuscript.

Place	Date	Hour	Summary of Events and Information	Remarks and references to Appendices
EPEHY	May 11		Pivot Engine for work on with started — waiting for cement. Sergeant LINNEY C.C. shot himself in the foot.	WS
	12		Division orders that all sappers be concentrated in communication trenches.	WS
	13		Well work building beds for Engine & tank. H.E. shell exploded made inrush on a cellar where part of No 3 section was billeted causing following casualties. KILLED Sappers A. ASHTON, S. BATES, W.D. BAKER, F. BARROWCLOUGH, J.W. HELLON, T.T. SHAW, W. SCOTT, J.C. THOMPSON, J. ROONEY, H. WILKINSON. WOUNDED (to hospital) Sappers J. McCANNAH, A. MANSFIELD, H. ROBERTS, H. STAVELEY, H. WATSON, S. YATES. WOUNDED (Remained at duty) Sapper E. FOWNES SHELL SHOCK (admitted to hospital) Sapper W. TOFT. SHELL FUMES & SHOCK (admitted to hospital) Corporal W. HIGGINS Sapper J. HALL Later. Sapper YATES died.	
	18		Mines details for work with No 3 Sec. 160th Tunnelling Cy. Also parties from H29 or 4X Coys detailed for same purpose returned to 429 Company Hq for recommendation of stations. Evans	WS WS

Army Form C. 2118.

WAR DIARY
or:
INTELLIGENCE SUMMARY.
(Erase heading not required.)

Instructions regarding War Diaries and Intelligence Summaries are contained in F. S. Regs., Part II. and the Staff Manual respectively. Title pages will be prepared in manuscript.

Place	Date	Hour	Summary of Events and Information	Remarks and references to Appendices
EPEHY	May 14		Work last night on dug outs for the enemy, in sunken road leading from EPEHY towards St. EMILIE. Big storm spoiled the work. R.E. officers of the 2nd Cavalry Division arrived to go round works prior to taking over	
	" 15	2.30pm	Buried the 11 men killed yesterday	
	" 16		Capt. N. ALLARD R.E. reported to duty from attachment H.Q. 127 Inf Bde. Reinforcement of 11 sappers dispatched to the Composite Field Squadron 2nd	
	" 18		Handed over held works last night to Composite Field Squadron 2nd Cavalry Division.	
VILLERS- FAUCON	" 19	4.30pm	Left EPEHY	
		8.15pm	Arrived. Billetted in Sugar Refinery	
	" 19		Lieut. G.E.T. Jones reported at DESSART WOOD for duty with his Coy.	
FINS	" 20	1.0 pm	Left	
		4.15 pm	Arrived	
"	" 21		Gas Parades. Lectures & practice under Coy. Gas N.C.O.	
DESSART WOOD	" 22	2.30pm	Left	
	" "	3.15pm	Arrived	
	" 23	7.0 am	No. 1 Coy. & 1 Section LAMFORD proceeded in Lt Mainchain & R Mainchain lorries attached to Btn. for YPRES and No. 2 Section with 9 Mainchains to BERTINCOURT, for Divisional work	
	" 24		42 Div. HQ. now being at YPRES. Coln. working nightly on wiring parties showing. Exta duty	

Army Form C. 2118.

WAR DIARY
-OF-
INTELLIGENCE SUMMARY.
(Erase heading not required.)

Instructions regarding War Diaries and Intelligence Summaries are contained in F. S. Regs., Part II. and the Staff Manual respectively. Title pages will be prepared in manuscript.

Place	Date 1917	Hour	Summary of Events and Information	Remarks and references to Appendices
DESSART WOOD	Aug 24		The day in Battalion HQrs	WS
	26		No 1 Section of Manchester Pioneers attached left GOUZEAUCOURT WOOD for YPRES to assist on dug outs.	WS
"	24	11.0 am	Capt ALLARD, Lt SINCLAIR HQrs with transport section left DESSART WOOD.	
BUS	"	1.0 pm	Arrived, drew tents made camp	
		3.0 pm	Lt JONES with No 4 Sections of Manchester Pioneers arrived from GOUZEAUCOURT WOOD.	WS
	28 to 31		Work on Hutis, water supply, and roads (crater filling) incinerators, sign-painting.	
	31		Strength of company 8 Officers, 180 O.Rs ranks. Infantry Pioneers 5th & 6th Bns attached 4 " 96 " " Manchester Regt. 12 282	

W Allard Capt.
O.C. 429 Coy R.E.

Army Form C. 2118.

WAR DIARY
INTELLIGENCE SUMMARY.
(Erase heading not required.)

Vol 5

of

429 Field Co. R.E. T.F.

from 1st to 30th JUNE 1917.

Volume 3.

Confidential

WAR DIARY or INTELLIGENCE SUMMARY

Army Form C. 2118.

Place	Date 1914	Hour	Summary of Events and Information	Remarks and references to Appendices
BUS FRANCE Map 1/40,000 O.24.b	June 1		Strength of Company: 8 officers, 196 other ranks. " " Infantry attached: " 4 " 96 " (5th, 6th, 7th & 8th Manchester) Total: 12 " 292 "	
"	2	9 am	Work continued on crew filling, water supply, engraining billets. No. 3 Sect & 7th M/Chr at BERTINCOURT, Nos 1 & 2 Sections and 6th & 8th M/Chr at YTRES. Draft of 34 Other Ranks reported from Nos. 4 (10) & 8 (1) Reinf. Coys RE. No. 4 Section 8th Manchester detached, left for YTRES.	WD
"	3		Work as yesterday, also resisting 427 Fld Coy on baths at BERTINCOURT. Draft of 3 men reported from No. 4 Reinforcement Coy RE. Company moved from BUS, YTRES & BERTINCOURT this afternoon and assembled & made camp at HAVRINCOURT WOOD, except location Map 57c P.18 Central. No. 4 Sect & 8th Manchester remained at YTRES.	WD
HAVRINCOURT WOOD P.18 Central	4		Camp reaching completion. Work handed over to Corps Roads Officers. Havrincourt filling point at YTRES commenced. Diversion of road at fallen church, BERTINCOURT, commenced. Trench tramway line jogged out beginning at PS a 2.4. Training begun and reach trolling commenced	WD
"	5		Men transferred to trench tramway line from K.31 c O.9. Surveying, clearing of trees & levelling of ground, commenced	WD
"	6		Lt Col A.N. LAWFORD reported from leave & resumed command of company. Work on trench tramways from K.31 c O.9.	WD
"	7		Work on trench tramways from K.31 c O.9.	WD

J.W. Manfred Clynes Lt Col RE

WAR DIARY
INTELLIGENCE SUMMARY
(Erase heading not required.)

Army Form C. 2118.

Place	Date 1917	Hour	Summary of Events and Information	Remarks and references to Appendices
HAVRINCOURT WOOD Map 57c P.18 Cad	June 8		Trench Tramways. Siding No.1 (K.31. C.0.9.) nearly completed. Communication Trench bridged. Progress made with levelling, clearing + tramways. Any slashers track along western edge of HAVRINCOURT WOOD detailed with entrench roots. Work in progress on 2nd line shelters. Working parties supplied by 12th Inf.Bde and transports by D.A.C. Work on Communications also begun. 4 new work as yesterday. 225 Yds of trench laid. Draft of 15 other ranks from No.4 Reinforcement Camp.R.E. All works carried on as previously.	W.H.
"	9			W.H.
"	10			W.H.
"	11			W.H.
"	12		Do. Also building of canteen at RUYAULCOURT commenced.	
"	13	8.p.m	2nd Lt. P. MOREY, East Lancs R.E. reported in reinforcement from 435 Res. Field Co. R.E. CARNARVON. Work continued as previously.	W.H.
"	14		Handed over work on Trench Tramways to 427 Fd.Co.R.E, and works on Dublin Shelters to 428 Field Co R.E	W.H.
"	15		Took over works in forward area from 4xx Fd.Co.R.E. Works on Aid post Brigade Battalion Headquarters, gunning shelter signal dug out, trolling posts &c Casualties: killed whilst at work in front line 442107 Sapper T. FLYNN. 442398 " C.W. HOLT. Wounded 442 426 R.E	W.H.

O.C. Hanford A.C.L 429 R.E

WAR DIARY
or
INTELLIGENCE SUMMARY
(Erase heading not required.)

Army Form C. 2118.

Place	Date	Hour	Summary of Events and Information	Remarks and references to Appendices
HAVRINCOURT WOOD 57° P 18 Cent	June 16		Works continued as yesterday	WD
"	17		Do.	WD
"	18		Do.	WD
"	19		Do.	WD
"	20		Do. Commenced erection of Pump Sunk for Well at TRESCAULT	WD
"	21		Engine delivered last night. Now in course of repair. Camouflage erected at Trescault Well, and Battalion Headquarters	WD
"	22		Do. Water Point at ST HUBERT. Commenced (Q 8 a 7.2)	WD
"	23		Do. ROMANI Commenced (Q 8 a 0.1)	WD
"	24		Do. Works on pumping	WD
"	26		Do. 2 Lieut T H DART RE. reported for duty (reinforcement) Also clearance of fallen trees at PLACE MORTEMARE on road	WD
"	28		Do. Completion of camouflage on the NETZ - TRESCAULT Road from PLACE MORTEMARE (Q 8 C 05)	WD
"	30		Bn. HQrs hut completed. Listening set dug out completed to pioneers requirements	WD
			Strength of Coy.—	
			" attached Infantry (15th 16th 17th 18th Manchesters)	10 officers 222 OR
				1 " 113 "
			Total	14 " 335 "

Stanhope Lt Col
429. CO RE.

Army Form C. 2118.

WAR DIARY
or
INTELLIGENCE SUMMARY.

Vol 6

429 Field Co. R.E.

JULY 1917.

from 1st to 31st.

Volume 3.

Army Form C. 2118.

WAR DIARY
or
INTELLIGENCE SUMMARY
(Erase heading not required.)

Place	Date 1917	Hour	Summary of Events and Information	Remarks and references to Appendices
HAVRINCOURT WOOD	July 1		Strength of Company 10 Officers 222 Other ranks	
			" " " Infantry attached 4 " 143 " (5th,6th,7th,8th Manchesters	Mnchs
				9/4th E. Lancs & 9th/10th Manchester)
			14 " 365 "	
"	2		Following works continued by R.E. Infantry attached. — Drainage of Trenches, C.T.'s. Clearing roads &c	
"	3		Works as yesterday except work on TRESCAULT road hindered by shell fire	Mnchs
"			Work in C.T's delayed by hostile shell fire. Road Repairs. Japanese Baths completed. "T" trade drains &c	Mnchs
"	4		One Officer & 5 OR of 58 Div. R.E. reported prior to taking over Metzinville Trenches & Roads Camouflaged (screen) Other works as before	Mnchs
"	6		2nd Cpl W CAKEBREAD wounded by gun shot. Handed over to 503rd Field Coy R.E. dugouts	Mnchs
"	7	4.0 pm	Coy paraded for inspection by Brig. Genl. Schrieber C.E. III Corps	Mnchs
		6.30 pm	Coy moved to YPRES	
			[signature]	

WAR DIARY
or
~~INTELLIGENCE SUMMARY~~
(Erase heading not required.)

Army Form C. 2118.

Place	Date 1917.	Hour	Summary of Events and Information	Remarks and references to Appendices
YTRES	July 8	3.30pm	Left for BARASTRE	Jw.B
BARASTRE	"	5.0pm	Arrived	Jw.B
"	9	8.0am	Left for ACHIET-LE-PETIT being inspected on moving from BARASTRE by G.O.C. 17 Army.	Jw.B
ACHIET-LE-PETIT	"	12 noon	Arrived	Jw.B
"	10		Fitting up camps of 127 Bde, ADMS hut, Int Bathe, A Office 42 Div & other small RE works viz work at Colyseum (CRATER).	Jw.B
"	11		As yesterday	Jw.B
"	13		Small works as before. Lt B.T.M.L. BOGLE M.C. reported from 437 Fd Coy. 2/Lt F.H. DART left for 437 Coy. Attached infantry returned to own units.	Jw.B
"	14		All works already completed	Jw.B
"	16		Training scheme commenced RE works, Infantry training, musketry, Organized games. Coy Sports on 20th July	Jw.B
"	20.			Jw.B
"	21 &		Training Coy moved to BEAUMONT-HAMEL at 11.30 am for Bridging schemes	Jw.Bogle

WAR DIARY
INTELLIGENCE SUMMARY

Army Form C. 2118.

(Erase heading not required.)

Place	Date	Hour	Summary of Events and Information	Remarks and references to Appendices
ACHIET le PETIT	1917 July 24	12 noon	Coy arrived from BEAUMONT-HAMEL having not slept at 9.0 a.m. having completed short training in Pontoon & Trestle Bridges, Foot Bridge & Pontoon Rafts, using equipment of 417 Fd.S.Co. Own equipment last 7 days spent in training. half Infantry half RE works. Brigade Divisional Sports also took place during this period.	Jn.18
	31.		Divisional R.E. wiring shooting football competition. Wiring shooting & final round football won by 419 Field Coy. Strength of Company. Officers - 9, other ranks - 213	Jn.18
			Attached { Brigade Workshop (Infantry) - 6 Interpreter 1 RAMC 1 - 9 } 22 4 CRE 4th Div Detached { Hospital (base + Area) - 2 Courses - 2 Harcourt (4th Army school) - 1 Albert (Cooking) - 1 } Lieut W.M. Rahn Struck off 6 16 20 2	

A6945. Wt. W14422/M1160 350,000 12/16 D. D. & L. Forms/C.2118/14.

Jn.18 Bogle
Lieut
M.R. 4th Div RE

Confidential

Army Form C. 2118.

WAR DIARY
or
INTELLIGENCE SUMMARY.
(Erase heading not required.)

Vol 7

429 FIELD COY R.E.

August 1917

Volume 3

Army Form C. 2118.

WAR DIARY
INTELLIGENCE SUMMARY.
(Erase heading not required.)

Place	Date 1917	Hour	Summary of Events and Information				Remarks and references to Appendices
				Officers	O.Ran.	randm.	total	
ACHIET-LE-PETIT	Aug 1		Strength of Company	9	213		69	
			Attached Interpreter 1 RamC 1		2			
			Standby (Bde Workshop)		6	RSM	70	
				9	221	6		
			detached					
			HQ 47 Div RE		1			
			Hospital (in Brit Open)		2			
			On leave UK		15			
			HQ Gen. Signals		1			
			Courses 4th Army Sigl School Attd.		1			Jn 18.
			4th army Infy School Heencourt		1			
			Ration Strength		6	201	69	
	20		The past 20 days have been spent in training ourselves for the offensive including carrying parties laying out trenches, strong points etc. wiring, gas drill, Bangalore & improvised Torpedoes &c, including one night scheme on the 4th August and 2 Brigade field days on the 9th & 19th of August. Instruction has

WAR DIARY
INTELLIGENCE SUMMARY.
(Erase heading not required.)

Army Form C. 2118.

Place	Date	Hour	Summary of Events and Information	Remarks and references to Appendices
Achiet le Petit	21		Also been given to Officers & other ranks of infantry of the 127th Infty Bde on wiring. The Company were inspected by the CRE 42 Div on the 11th. The competition in rapid wiring & shooting football between the Field Coys of 42 DN were won by this Company. The VI Corps sports were held on 18/8/17 & attended by the Coy.	Jm.IB Jm.IB
	21	9.0 pm	Left	Jm.IB
BOUZINCOURT nr ALBERT	"	2.30 am	Arrived	Jm.IB
"	23	7.30 am	Left - entrained at AVELUY at 10.30	
POPERINGHE Belgium	"	11.0 pm	Arrived	Jm.IB
	25		1 Officer & 26 other ranks reported from each Bn. of 127th Infty Bde viz 5th, 6th, 7th & 8th Manchester	Jm.IB
	28		Lt. J. E. EASTWOOD, reinforcement, reported for duty	Jm.IB
	29	10.30 am	Left	
VLAMERTINGHE	"	2.15 pm	Arrived	Jm.IB
	31		Works - Repairing billets & hospitals &c	Jm.IB

WAR DIARY
INTELLIGENCE SUMMARY
(Erase heading not required.)

Army Form C. 2118.

Place	Date	Hour	Summary of Events and Information	Remarks and references to Appendices
VLAMERTINGHE	31		HQrs, No 1, No 2, Section to YPRES Transport Section No 4 Section to REFPARK BRANDHOEK (Note No 3 Section already in YPRES having proceeded there from POPERINGHE on 26.8.17 to work on shelters & dugouts)	Jn 18
"	"			
YPRES	"		2/Lt. CARTER wounded in action	
"	"		Strength of Coy Rank (s) Intrepeter(i) O.R. Horses	
			Infantry attached 6 110 71	
			8 3	
			4 104	
			Bde workshop infantry 6	
			4/Divl Signals 1	
			17 mancreaders awaiting transfer 1	
			17 325 71	
			Attached	
			Hospital RE & Infantry (2) 1 — 10	
			Leave to UK 7	
			HQ RE 1 — 3 . 1	
			4/Divl Signals 1	
			10 . 30 t. 70	

Arthur Murphy
Lt. Col. R.E.
for Capt
for Fusiliers
OC 29 RE

Vol 8

WAR DIARY

429 Field Coy R.E.

September 1917

Volume 3

Confidential
ORIGINAL

WAR DIARY
INTELLIGENCE SUMMARY

Army Form C. 2118.

Place	Date	Hour	Summary of Events and Information	Remarks and references to Appendices
YPRES	1917 Sept. 1		Strength of Company including transport lines at Brandhoek. O OR Horses 8 209 71	
			Machine Workshop 1, RAMC 2, Bn Workshop 6, 42 DIV Signals 1	
			17 Manchesters arriving hangar 1 — 11	
			127 Inf Bde Pioneers attached 4 104	
			Totals 12 3 x 1 71	
			Hospital 1- RE 1, OR 8 Bn Pioneers 2	
			Leave to UK 1 10	
			Interview in France 7	
			NO 4 DIV RE 1 1	
			3 1 4 DN SIGS 1 4 1	
			Coy Ration Strength 10 303 70	Jn CB
"	2		Work on Elephant shelter for billets in YPRES	
			No 3 Section one Coy 16 Manchesters on Elephant shelter in YPRES. Nos 1 + 2 Sect +	
			2 Section and Infantry worked Pioneer Games lines relieving 61 + drawing	
			augments making shelter for troops. No 4 Section at BRANDHOEK	
			RE Park Capt F.E. DUTTON rejoins from Base ROUEN	
			2nd Lieut P. MORREY sick to hospital	Jn CB

Lieut P. MORREY

WAR DIARY
INTELLIGENCE SUMMARY
(Erase heading not required.)

Army Form C. 2118.

Place	Date	Hour	Summary of Events and Information	Remarks and references to Appendices
YPRES	3		Work as yesterday	JMcIB
	4		6 my F.E. BUTTON posted to 478 Coy R.E. & left for that Coy	JMcIB
	5		do	JMcIB
	6		No 4 Section (16th manoeuvre attached) arrived from R.E. Park BRANDHOEK	JMcIB
			3 Section down to BRANDHOEK	
	7 to 12		Nos 1, 2, & 4 Section 5, 6, 7, & 8th manoeuvres attached on clearing drainage drops	JMcIB
			dugouts	
	12		No 3 Section joined Coy in YPRES	JMcIB
	13		All working in dug dugouts in the line. "JAMES" dugout completed & tent	JMcIB
	14		As yesterday and also shelter in trenches at "HUSSAR" farm for sgs BkRA	JMcIB
	15		All on dugouts. Two power pumps received	JMcIB
	16		2 Lieut D.C. CHAPMAN joined from 427 Coy R.E.	JMcIB
R.E. PARK BRANDHOEK	16	2pm	morning on dugouts. Moved at midday arrived	JMcIB
"	17	Dawn	left	
BUSSEBOUM		2pm	arrived	JMcIB

WAR DIARY
or
INTELLIGENCE SUMMARY.

(Erase heading not required.)

Army Form C. 2118.

Instructions regarding War Diaries and Intelligence Summaries are contained in F. S. Regs., Part II. and the Staff Manual respectively. Title pages will be prepared in manuscript.

Place	Date	Hour	Summary of Events and Information	Remarks and references to Appendices
BUSSEBOOM	18		Infantry training, bayonet fighting, rifle exercises &C	Jnl8.
"	19	12.30pm	Left	Jnl8
POPERINGHE	"	2pm	Arrived at former camp, East of POPERINGHE	
"	20	7.30 am	Left by Route March with 127 Bde.	
WINNEZEELE AREA	20	12 noon	Arrived. Billeted bivouacy at L Ferme.	Jnl8
"	21	12.30pm	Transport left by road	Jnl13
"	22	7.00 am	Marched to Embarking point Pt 127 by L/Bde H.Q.	
"	"	9.0 am	Left by Motor Bus	
COXYDE	"	2pm	Arrived at CANADA CAMP	Jnl8
"	"	11.30	pm Transport arrived at CANADA CAMP.	Jnl8
"	23		Infantry training	
NIEUPORT BAINS	24		Coy. moved to NIEUPORT BAINS cellars in small parties by road to LAITERIE ROYALE (dumps by Coxyde)	
			C.T. to Cellars of NIEUPORT BAINS	
			No 2 Section billeted with 16 Inf. attached in BROKEN HILL dug outs nr.	
			LAITERIE ROYALE. Transport lines moved to OOST DUNKERKE BAINS	Jnl8
			Took over work & billets from 432 Field Coy R.E.	

WAR DIARY
INTELLIGENCE SUMMARY
(Erase heading not required.)

Army Form C. 2118.

Place	Date 1917	Hour	Summary of Events and Information	Remarks and references to Appendices
NIEUPORT BAINS	Sept 25		Maintenance of camouflage screens on N.B. road	
			Endeavour of Tunnelling at MGE C.9 in two shifts	
			Inspecting & Stabling MGEs (12) Repair POPLAR O.P.	
			Construction of Gun emplacement at 330 R.F.A.	
			N.Z.R.A. Hdqrs. Cherry Huyot Reversed of roof	
			Stabling Ullar Both Rooms 9 A.D.S. Kilgoul & Buxton.	
"	26		Completing tunnel on N.B. road	Jn.13
"	27		As yesterday	Jn.13
"	28		Re stacking and maintaining trenches, sandbagging filling &c.	Jn.13
			Blankets & coverings in Reserve Major Dumps	
"	29		Transport Lines moved to MORAY CAMP CORIULE BAINS.	Jn.13
			No. 9 Team Gun Breastwork at K.13.d.9.3.	
"	30		No. 2 Section working old road by N.B.O.2 in Pack Carts & Limbered wagons &c.	Jn.13

Army Form C. 2118.

WAR DIARY
INTELLIGENCE SUMMARY.
(Erase heading not required.)

Place	Date 1917	Hour	Summary of Events and Information	Remarks and references to Appendices
NIEUPORT-BAINS	Sept 30		Strength of Company	
			Officers Knott, Lt Morrison, 4 2/Lt Sequiera	O or Morrison 1
			Lee Poirier (129 Infantry Bn)	NCO 107 F7.
				R 75
			Attached	
			Hospital R.E.	4 164
			H.Q 42 Austrl E	12 3.19 75
			Leave to UK	1. 19
			" " France	1 4 1
			H.Q on Siege	1 21
			R.E Park	1
				2
			On 21.1/17 March Poirier attached whereabouts unknown	1
			but believed to be in hospital.	
			Ration Strength	9 241 74

Jn. Knott E
Capt
2nd 424th RE

WAR DIARY
or
INTELLIGENCE SUMMARY.
(Erase heading not required.)

Army Form C. 2118.

429 FIELD COY. R.E.

OCTOBER 1917

Volume 3.

Confidential
Original

Army Form C. 2118.

WAR DIARY
INTELLIGENCE SUMMARY
(Erase heading not required.)

Place	Date	Hour	Summary of Events and Information	Remarks and references to Appendices
NIEUPORT BAINS	1917 Oct. 1		Strength of Company	
				Officers O.R.
				8 205
			Attached R.A.M.C. 1, Bde Workshop 6, 42 Divl Signals 1	8
			127th Infantry Brigade Pioneers	4 10
				Officers OR
			Weather	12 214
			Hospital R.E. 1 1st Infantry 4	1 18
			HQ 42 Divl RE 1, 74th, Leave 1, 422	
			42 Divl RE Park 2 OR Signal Coy 1 OR	2 29 3 41
			Total Ration Strength	9 240
			Work on Maintenance of trenches, filling in Blankets, working on Reserve Main Tanks, Lewis Gun Portwork, &c	
			Lts HUGHES & 9 O.R. to FURNES to renewing instruction	
			Sergt 2/ E & man on Transport Lines making Pack Crates &c	
	5		Work continued as on 1st Oct	
	6	6 am	Advance party to NIEUPORT to go round work	
			Coy moved in October to new billets at NIEUPORT took over from the 118 Field Coy R.E. Work at NIEUPORT BAINS handed over to 233 Field Coy R.E.	

WAR DIARY or INTELLIGENCE SUMMARY

Army Form C. 2118.

(Erase heading not required.)

Place	Date 1917 Oct.	Hour	Summary of Events and Information	Remarks and references to Appendices
NIEUPORT	6		2/Lt. T.Y. HUGHES slightly wounded and Cpl S.C. MORT & Pnr D. WRIGHT killed by shell	
	7		Work on Bridges over YSER canal stranded. Patrols by night. Infantry mainly employed in carrying parties. Engineers ft. Haulaging dumps &c	
			Sgt A. JOHNSON slightly wounded	
	8		Standard crew moved to NEWFOUNDLAND Camp S. of COXYDE	
			Sub sec building ramp at M.28.c.9.2. Sheet 1v Belgium	
			Repairs to Bry Billets Nieuport to No. 23 Bridge	
	9		Ditto, also Nieuport to No. 31 Bridge. Building reinforced concrete Bomb at Pier at Bridge No M. Clearing wreckage from VAUXHALL PUTNEY	
			(CROWDER broken by shell fire Repaired) same day	
	10	10.35 am	CROWDER broken by shell & foot bridge alongside (67)	
			" CROWDER damaged (repair) at 11.35 am	
	2.30 pm		" " 3.50 pm	
	8.30 "		" " 9.10 pm	

WAR DIARY

INTELLIGENCE SUMMARY

(Erase heading not required.)

Army Form C. 2118.

Place	Date 1917	Hour	Summary of Events and Information	Remarks and references to Appendices
NIEUPORT	Oct 10	7.15 pm	VAUXHALL broken by shell repaired by 8.8 pm	
	11		Moral patrols which carry on daily also Paris on No 29	
	11	9.0 am	Reinforced Concrete bag for Dam No 66 continues	
		8.40 pm	PUTNEY damaged by shell repaired by 11 am	
			" 9.10 pm	
	12		Spr. A.E. ROBBINS Wounded. Other work continued	
	13		Usual works. Sapper J.T. McCARTHY slightly wounded	
		6.15 am	VAUXHALL Damaged. Repaired by 6.10 pm	
		11.5 pm	CRONDER " "	
	14	11.00 am	CRONDER repaired. Works as usual	
		7.15 pm	VAUXHALL damaged. 4.30 pm PUTNEY damaged Repaired by 11.10 pm	
	15	10.30 am	VAUXHALL damaged + damaged again at 1 pm. 2nd Col.	
	15/16	12 MID	PUTNEY damaged W. HYNES wounded taken on DAM 66	
	16	2.30 am	" repaired	
		1.30	am VAUXHALL repaired	
		4.30 pm	CRONDER damaged + repaired at 8.30 pm	
	15/16	Night	Accville truck laid to carriage of material to DAM 66	

Army Form C. 2118.

WAR DIARY
INTELLIGENCE SUMMARY.
(Erase heading not required.)

Instructions regarding War Diaries and Intelligence Summaries are contained in F. S. Regs., v art. II. and the Staff Manual respectively. Title pages will be prepared in manuscript.

Place	Date 1917	Hour	Summary of Events and Information	Remarks and references to Appendices
NEUPORT	Oct 16		Lt. J. ENTWISTLE from ~~reinforcements~~ Base	
	16/17	night	Shrapnel 66 handed over to 427 Fd Coy. 1 man to-day	
	17		Repairs to Orderly Room Nissen damaged by shell fire	
		3.45 am	CROWDER damaged and repaired by S.17 pm	
		4.50 "	No 22 Bridge damaged & repaired by 6.5 pm	
	18		Party of 6 O.R. lent to 427 Coy R.E. for work in front line	
			Lieut C.E.T. JONES and Lt. J. ENTWISTLE to 428"	
		1.0 pm	PUTNEY damaged from 427 Coy & 5.20pm Shell fire prevented	
			9 again at 5.20pm left to 10 days leave to U.K.	
			Capt J M L'BOGUE left to repair until next day	
		2.45 pm	VAUXHALL damaged	
	19		3 O.R. to A771 RFA for supervisor of concrete emplacements to	
			Fort "K" O-P commenced in horses at M 28 C 10.95 Sheet 5	
			Lieut J.V. HUGHES reported from hospital	
		3.0 am	VAUXHALL repairs	
		3.30 pm	VAUXHALL again damaged & again repaired at 9.10 pm	
		4.0 am	PUTNEY repaired	
		12.20 pm	PUTNEY repaired	

WAR DIARY
INTELLIGENCE SUMMARY
(Erase heading not required.)

Army Form C. 2118.

Place	Date 1917	Hour	Summary of Events and Information	Remarks and references to Appendices
NIEUPORT	20		Usual work. Clearing tracks & approaches of Bridges	
	21		Ferry between VAUXHALL & CROWDER Bridges (M.Y.S. & 3.7) commenced.	
			& Fetch Nail strip for same commenced. 25 Cyclists working parties from various units	
			Normal shell fire on VAUXHALL, CROWDER & PUTNEY all day	
			Several Wounded at train	
	22		Bombing dump (M34 & 4A) shells exploding - some damage	
			Ferry as usual & cyclists working party at night	
		4.30pm	CROWDER DAMAGED. repaired by 10pm 23/10/17	
		4.20pm	PUTNEY damaged repaired by 6.0pm	
		10.0pm	" " 1.0am 23/10/17	
	23		Usual work, including Bridge approaches, ferry "K" OP	
			Ferry &c. Lieut HUGHES to Nieuport line to-day	
		6.40am	VAUXHALL repaired	
		2.X am	CROWDER damages 9.0am at 4.15. Repaired by 4.45 am	
		4.15	PUTNEY repaired at 6.30pm	
	24	10.15am	CROWDER damaged by shell repaired by 10.33 am	

WAR DIARY
INTELLIGENCE SUMMARY
(Erase heading not required.)

Army Form C. 2118.

Place	Date	Hour	Summary of Events and Information	Remarks and references to Appendices
NIEUPORT	Oct 24	1.15 pm	CROWDER damages repaired by 7.30 pm	
		2.15 pm	" No 23 damaged	
		3.0 pm	VAUXHALL damaged	
	25	7.0 pm	VAUXHALL repaired	
		2.45 am	No 46 & 56 damages + repaired (both) at 9.50 am	
		9.0 am	No 25 damaged	
"	26	2.0 pm	" " repaired	
		3.15 pm	CROWDER damages repaired by 10.53 pm	
			Ferry at M.X.h.3.7. in advance. Ferry commenced at M.X.C.H.2.r Approaches being prepared. Raft already launched rcable b.0 (24/4/16)	
"	27		2/Lr H.T. PAUL (reinforcement) reported for duty	
		2.15 pm	No 22 damaged & repaired by 4 pm	
		8.0 pm	No 23 repaired. Passage in Rockwall for new ferry commenced	
"	28	1.15 am	PUTNEY damaged & repaired by 5.30 am	
		3.0 am	VAUXHALL " " 9.30 am	
			Const "KOP" demolition in Rock Wall and minor works continued	

/ WAR DIARY
or
INTELLIGENCE SUMMARY.

Army Form C. 2118.

Place	Date	Hour	Summary of Events and Information	Remarks and references to Appendices
NIEUPORT	Oct 29		Works as yesterday.	
		5.15pm	61st VAUXHALL damage & repairs by 9 pm	
		5.30pm	No 76 damaged	
	30	4.0am	" " repaired.	
		3.0pm	PUTNEY damaged.	
	31	4.0am	" " repaired.	
			Other works as usual	
		3.15pm	No 76 22 damaged	
			Sapper G.COLES slightly wounded, remained duty. Sergt HIGGINS to Hospital (? Shell shock) after shell burst near him	
			Billets slightly damaged by heavy shell fire during the afternoon	
			Strength of Coy	officers O.R.
				10 191
			Attached HQ RE 1 & 2 Burma 3 O & OY. OR. Workshops 6 O & Signal Coy 1 R 3	13 196
			Attached HQ RE 1 & 3 Hospital 1 & 2 Leave 1.19	
			Bridging tours 1. MRTD 3 Duck R Pk 3 Signals 1	3 32
			Return Strength	10 . 267

Army Form C. 2118.

WAR DIARY
of
INTELLIGENCE SUMMARY.
(Erase heading not required.)

Vol 10

429 FIELD CO
ROYAL ENGINEERS

November 1917

VOLUME 3

WAR DIARY
INTELLIGENCE SUMMARY
(Erase heading not required.)

Army Form C. 2118.

Place	Date	Hour	Summary of Events and Information	Remarks and references to Appendices
NIEWPORT	1917 Nov 1		Strength of Coy Officers OR %	
			Modest [Radio 1 or 127 Infy Bde Gp.uio 3 Offs 96 OR, 9 191	off
			(Signal Coy 1 OR " Workshop 6 OR 3 104	off
			12 295	off
			0. OR	off
			Wacken HQ+DivSigCo. 3 OR. Hospital 1 off 4 6 OR.	off
			Leave to UK 1st Bde 20 OR. Bridging Crew 2 OR.	off
			Ghelware 1 OR. RFA n/Bou 3 OR	off
			42 Divn REPart 3 OR 4 Divn Signals 1 OR 2 39	off
			Ration Strength 10 256	off
			Works — Fort K OP. , Aerial Ropeway across the Marshes Yser Canal	off
			Bridge Patrols & Bridge repairs as usual.	off
		2	No 1 Section + 46 Bttn Manchesters begun from Back Ave. No 2 Section Vs NIEWPORT	off
			Attacked No 6 Back Ave	off
		3	Work carried on at Nieuport M & G55.65 when dock wall hit now	off
			been cut through. Steps made for landing O.og.	off
			CRONDER damaged 7.30pm. Repaired 6.30pm, VAUXHALL 10.30am repaired 5.30pm	off
			No 21 Bridge 8am slightly, repaired 8.15am.	off

Army Form C. 2118.

WAR DIARY
INTELLIGENCE SUMMARY
(Erase heading not required.)

Place	Date 1917 Nov	Hour	Summary of Events and Information	Remarks and references to Appendices
NIEUPORT	4		Observations as usual. Brigade Main Scheme commenced. Slight damage	OC/11
			Nos. 28 & 29 repaired. VAUXHALL damaged 4.20 pm CROWDER damaged 4.20 pm	OC/11
			Bridging dump nearly shelled	OC/11
"	5		VAUXHALL repaired from CROWDER repaired 9.0 am	OC/11
			Soft K. O.P. Main Scheme. Aerial repairing to no avail	OC/11
"	6		Cpy Billets shelled two direct hits – no casualties	OC/11
"	7		Capt R. BRIGHMORE, Sapper J. RYLANCE & J. BENNETT wounded the military medal (42 Div R.O. 793) wounded R.E.M. hole in roadway of BRIDGE of SIGHS. Repair	OC/11
"	8		Sapper H. GALPINE killed by shell whilst on patrol on CROWDER bridge	OC/11
			PUTNEY slightly damaged repaired	OC/11
"	9		No 2 Section w/s moved Advanced Dump nucleus No. 3 + 1/8 who proceed	OC/11
			to billets in back area. No 46 Bridge damaged 5 am	OC/11
"	10		PUTNEY VAUXHALL slightly damaged at and F.O. am repaired soon afterwards	OC/11
"	11		No 46 bridge repaired by 5 am	OC/11
"	12		As usual. Also working parties carrying dumps & submerging dumps up	OC/11
			to required strength in bridge parts.	OC/11
"	13		As usual. The 3 man wounded of 2nd Bn R.F.A. reported	OC/11
			2 Lieut J.F.H. NICOLSON awarded the MILITARY CROSS (42 Div R.O. 806 12/11/17)	OC/11

WAR DIARY
INTELLIGENCE SUMMARY
(Erase heading not required.)

Army Form C. 2118.

Place	Date 1917	Hour	Summary of Events and Information	Remarks and references to Appendices
NIEUPORT	Nov 14		AERIAL ROPEWAY nearly completed. Other works carried on as usual	O.W.
—	15		Ammunition transported across the MARITIME YSER CANAL by the Aerial Ropeway. FORT K O.P. complete	O.W.
			PUTNEY damaged 8.30 am	O.W.
—	16		No 3 Section r/l/c withdrawn relieves No. 4 4/17 Mtn detachment	O.W.
			No 4 4/17 to back area	O.W.
			2/Lt A.N.LAWFORD to HOWDNE R.E. to br	O.W.
			A/CRE during absence on leave of Lt Col D.G. MAC. INNES	O.W.
			PUTNEY repaired 9.0 am. Ammunition transported across Aerial	O.W.
			ropeway during the night (British Ammunition being withdrawn	stuff
			from front line)	stuff
—	18		4th Coy 58th DN French Army arrived & took over all billets	stuff
			Capt J M L BOGLE sick to Hospital Lieut C.E.T. TONES reported from 428 Coy	O.W.
			PUTNEY damaged 11.45 am, CROWDER at 3.10 pm VAUXHALL at 3.10 pm	O.W.
			" repaired 5.0 pm " at 4.45 pm " at 3.10 pm	
			" " " 4.45 pm. New bridge	
			repaired under shell fire to enable the Lancashire Fusiliers	
			(125th Infty Bde) to withdraw from front line for the French	
			relieving Battalions to take over	

Army Form C. 2118.

WAR DIARY
—of—
INTELLIGENCE SUMMARY.
(Erase heading not required.)

Instructions regarding War Diaries and Intelligence Summaries are contained in F. S. Regs., Part II. and the Staff Manual respectively. Title pages will be prepared in manuscript.

Place	Date 1917	Hour	Summary of Events and Information	Remarks and references to Appendices
NIEUPORT	Nov 18	6.0 pm	No 1 Section infantry marched to COXYDE	CBG
		11.30 pm	Enemy patrol taken prisoner MARITIME YSER bridge	
	19	1.30 am	" " the FIVE BRIDGES	CBG
		3.0 am	All our patrols withdrawn	
		6.0 pm	Coy marched to COXYDE leaving 2nd Lieut J.F.H NICOLSON, M.C. R.E.	CBG
			to hand over the works	
COXYDE	"	10.0 am	Entrained with 125th Infy Bde	CBG
OXEM	"	4.0 pm	Arrived & billeted	CBG
TETEGHEM	20	9.0 am	Left by Route March with 125th Infy Bde	CBG
WYLDER (WORMHOUDT AREA)	"	3.0 pm	Arrived & billeted	CBG
"	21	9.30 am	Left by Route March with 125th Infy Bde	CBG
ZERMEZEELE (WORMHOUDT AREA)	"	11.30 am	Arrived & billeted	CBG
"	22	9.0 am	Left by Route March with 125th Infy Bde	CBG
LE NIEPPE (STAPLE AREA)	"	2.0 pm	Arrived & billeted	CBG
"	23	9.15 am	Left by Route March with 125th Infy Bde	CBG
LA ROUPIE (Nr AIRE)	"	1.30 pm	Arrived & billeted in 127th Infy Bde Area	CBG
"	24/25		Rested. Feet attended to &c	

WAR DIARY
INTELLIGENCE SUMMARY

Army Form C. 2118.

Place	Date 1917 Nov	Hour	Summary of Events and Information	Remarks and references to Appendices
LA ROUPIE	26	9.0 am	Left by route march with 127th Inf Bde. Lt Nicolson + 4 NCOs sent to GORRE (nr BETHUNE) to reconnoitre new work	
MT BERNENCHON	"	2.0 pm	Arrived – billeted	
"	27	12.0 Noon	Left by Route March	
GORRE	"	3.0 pm	Arrived + billeted in GORRE Brewery, taking same over from 130 Field Coy R.E.	
			Working parties are sent to front line from this billet	
			The work consists of Machine Gun Emplacements, Trench Mortar Emplacements, Repair + upkeep of trenches, Dugouts for Batln + Bgd. HQrs., +C. Works things over to-day	
"	28/30		Works carried on as taken over	
	30		Strength of Coy — officers 8 O.R. 196	
			Attached R.A.M.C. 1 O.R., 127th Bde Pnr A.O. 101 O.R. 127 Bde Wksps 6 O.R.	
			H.Qrs Signals 1 O.R. 408 Coy ASC 2 O.R. Bomb Party 8 O.R. 5 O.R.	
			Tramway Party 10. 15 O.R. Labour Coy a/d 5 O.R. 5 136	
			Detached HQRE a/dn 10 & 4 O.R. Hospital 10 & 2 O.R. 13. 335	
			Leave to U.K. 28 O.R. + Army bySchool 10 1 pn Legnd Coy 1 O.R. 3 37	
			Ration Strength for Front + Rear = Ration Strength 10. 295	

Army Form C. 2118.

WAR DIARY

INTELLIGENCE SUMMARY.
(Erase heading not required.)

429 FIELD COY RE

DECEMBER 1917

Volume 3

WAR DIARY
INTELLIGENCE SUMMARY

(Erase heading not required.)

Army Form C. 2118.

Reference Maps. France. Sheets. 36A.SE, 36SW.
36A.NE, 36B.NW. 1/20,000
36B.NE.

Place	Date	Hour	Summary of Events and Information				Remarks and references to Appendices
				Officers.	O.Rs.	Horses.	
GORRE.	1-12-17		Strength of Company.	8	195.	73.	
			Attached: 127th Infty Bde. Pioneers 4 off. 100 O.R.				
			" " Bde. Workshop.	6			
			" 42nd Divl Train.	2.	4horses.		
			" Signals.	1.			
			" Tramway Party.	1.	15.		
			71st Labour Coy.	5.			
			Burial Party	1.	5.	4.	
			R.A.M.C.		13.	330.	77.
			Detached. H.Q. Divl R.E.	1 off. 4 O.R. 2 horses			
			Hospital	1. 2.			
			Leave to U.K.	nil.			
			4th Army Infty School. 1. 1.				
			42nd Divl Signals. 1.				
			Ration Strength	10	298.	75	
	4.12.17		Lt Col A.N. Sanford rejoined from a/CRE, 42 Divn on return from leave of Lt Col O.S. MacInnes, CMG. DSO. RE				
	1-12-17 to 11-12-17		Works in progress:- Emplacements for heavy T.M's; emplacements for 8 machine guns in FESTUBERT E. KEEP, shell-proof shelter for Battn H.Q. - Left Bde, Left Bde, gas proofing dugouts; protecting water tanks, fitting up new installation for Divl forward take (spray)				

WAR DIARY
or
INTELLIGENCE SUMMARY.

(Erase heading not required.)

Army Form C. 2118.

Place	Date	Hour	Summary of Events and Information	Remarks and references to Appendices
GORRE	1-13-17		Repairs to communication trenches, and maintenance of water supply. Pipe system. There are 3 of	
	11-12-17		the latter 2 being supplied by hand pumps pumping into a main reservoir, the other by an electrically driven pump.	
	11-12-17		Capt. A. N. WALKER, Adjt. to C.R.E. 170th Div? temporarily changed places with Lieut. J. T. HUGHES.	MW
	12-12-17		Horse lines of Company shelled in afternoon, believed by long range anti-aircraft guns firing	
			at our own aeroplanes flying low. Following casualties sustained:-	
			Killed. 442131. Dr B. JONES, 442154. Dr A. W. WALKER.	
			Wounded. 442050. Dr J. R. MULDOON. 442114. Dr S. FRANCE. 442075 Dr J. SNELSON	MW
			Horses. 4 killed (including 1 altets for shooting) 5 wounded, revacated.	
			Windy Corner R.E. Dump (A.14.a.9.8) lightly shelled in afternoon, following casualties occurred:-	
			Wounded. 442046 Sapper H. BURSLEM.	
			42262. Pte LUCAS, 71st Labour Coy. (attchd)	
	13-12-17		Capt. C. E. TURNER JONES commenced 14 days leave in U.K.	MW
	14-12-17		The Company was employed on work in left Bde Sector East of FESTUBERT Rd	
	to		A shell proof Batt Hdqrs was constructed for left Batn. This proved more difficult than	
	27-12-17		anticipated owing to its location and the presence of water. Machine Gun emplacements	
			for 8 guns were proceeded with and completed at S.26.c.8.7. Screening was maintained	MW

WAR DIARY or INTELLIGENCE SUMMARY

Army Form C. 2118.

Place	Date	Hour	Summary of Events and Information	Remarks and references to Appendices
GORRE	14-12-17		and the erection of new screens commenced where required. Communication trenches were repaired and technical assistance given to Infantry for repair of Front Line. One officer (Infantry Pioneers attached) was set apart for drainage work. Existing drains were weeded and cleared and new drains dug to connect up with main drains. Gauge posts were fixed to check the rise and fall of water level in the drains.	
	27-12-17		On the night of Bn. Area, Small "B" Type shelters were erected in the front line trench joining the various saps. This work was camouflaged and was able to be worked upon in daylight. Difficulty was experienced in the fixing of a long distance in which slates had to be carried from the trench tramway. Two Trench Mortar (6") emplacements at A.G.C.S. were continued and completed as far as R.E. work was concerned and a shelter (Light "C" Type) erected for the gun crews. The shell proofing of this shelter was not proceeded with owing to pressure of more urgent work. Right Battalion H.Qrs. was made one shellproof by the addition and extension of walls and a "C" Type shelter was also erected to be made shell proof by means of reinforced concrete. The provision of shell proof accommodation for the Support Battalion near Windy Corner was commenced and a good start made, but the work was then handed over to the Reserve Field Company.	MM

Army Form C. 2118.

WAR DIARY
or
INTELLIGENCE SUMMARY.
(Erase heading not required)

Place	Date	Hour	Summary of Events and Information	Remarks and references to Appendices
			Continued frost naturally interfered with all concrete work and thus materials for concreting were carried up in large quantities into the various sites to await the thaw. The forward R.E. Dumps at WINDY CORNER (A.14.a.9.8) and ESTAMINET CORNER (F.6.c.4.9) gradually became better stocked with all R.E. Stores and were linked up.	MM
	27-12-17		Lt Col A.N. LAWFORD commenced one month's leave in U.K.	MM
	28-12-17		Capt C.E. TOERNER JONES rejoined from leave in U.K.	MM
	29-12-17 to 31-12-17		The frost continued and work on clearing drains was stopped as a result the ice on some drainage canals being as much as 5" thick. Arrangements were made to start news jobs:- provision of shell-proof accommodation for 2 Coy HQ for the Left Batt.y and for a shelter for a wireless station near Kws Batt.n HQ. Three houses were not actually started this month. A start was made on constructing a shot-up specimen length of a communication trench (WOLFE ROAD - A.9.d.2.1) & means of interference by enemy shelling. But this was not completed this month owing to interference by enemy shelling. The 1/4th S. Lancs (Pioneer) Regt arrived in the area on the 29th and ½ company was allotted to this Coy company for work on trench maintenance. They began	

WAR DIARY
or
INTELLIGENCE SUMMARY.
(Erase heading not required.)

Army Form C. 2118.

Place	Date	Hour	Summary of Events and Information	Remarks and references to Appendices
GORRE	29-12-17	6	Work on the trenches in the at. Batt's sub-sector on the 31st this relieving a certain number of Sappers and attached infantry for other work. The 422nd Fd Co. R.E. also arrived and took on a fatigue in the area of the 429 R.E. On the 30th	CRE
	31-12-17		GIVENCHY KEEP was damaged by shell fire and repairs were undertaken	
	31-12-17		Strength of Company	O.R. / 74
			Attached 127 "Bde Inf Pioneers "4 off 100 O.R.	O.R. / 16
			" Pioneers Clerk 6	
			" Worksh/p 5	
			422nd Div Sig. Co 1	
			Burial Party 5	
			422nd Div "R.E Park Park 39	4 / 157
				11 / 353
			Details HQ R.E. 422nd Div 1	
			leave to U.K. 12	
			Hospital 8	
			422nd Div R.E Park 5	1 / 26
			Ratio Strength 10 327 74	

Army Form C. 2118.

WAR DIARY
INTELLIGENCE SUMMARY.
(Erase heading not required.)

Vol 12

429th Field Coy
Royal Engineers
January 1918
Volume 4

WAR DIARY

INTELLIGENCE SUMMARY

(Erase heading not required.)

Army Form C. 2118.

Reference Maps
France Sheets 36A S.E. 36 S.W.
36 B N.E. 36 C N.W. 1/20000

Place	Date	Hour	Summary of Events and Information			Remarks and references to Appendices
				Off.	O.R.	
GORRE	1-1-18		Strength of Company	4	109	
			Attached			
			127th Inf. Bde. Pioneers		26	
			RAMC		6	
			"13d. Morg.bfs		1	
			"Pioneer Clubs (junior)		5	
			42nd Div. Signal Co.		3	
			Brigade R.E.		9	
			42nd Div. R.E. Park Party	4	159	
			Detached			
			H.Q. R.E. 42nd Div.		2	
			Leave to U.K.		13	
			Hospital		7	
			Courses		5	
				Officers	O.R.	Horses
				7	198	74
				1	157	–
				11	355	74
					1	27
			Ration Strength	10	328	74
	1-1-18		Capt. AN WALKER returned to H.Q.R.E. to resume duties as Adjutant. Lieut. J.Y. HUGHES temporarily retained by C.R.E.			CBG
	3-1-18		Sgt. COOKE wounded by shell fire while on the works. Subsequently died of wounds.			CBG
	5-1-18		Lieut. J.Y. HUGHES returned to unit (from MS R.E.)			CBG
			No 2/1 Company of 1/4th (Pioneer) Bn. South Lancs Regt. began relieving SHETLAND			CBG
	1-1-18		Communication trench on the extreme left of the Brigade Sector. This trench			
	6		has fallen in & away too condition owing to the recent bring in. Some difficulty was			
	31-1-18		experienced on the trench in parts was so bad that on fine day a man could be seen			CBG
			by the enemy when standing upright in the trench. The parties were before sometimes			

WAR DIARY
INTELLIGENCE SUMMARY

(Erase heading not required.)

Army Form C. 2118.

Place	Date	Hour	Summary of Events and Information	Remarks and references to Appendices
GORRE	1-1-18		Intermittent MG enemy snipers by day. MG and shell and machine guns. Rather left small and few guns were slow.	
	31-1-18		On the 22nd a shot was made on one of the Lewis gun posts by Capt Bell & Lieut Richmond Trench Mortar Battery. It was made at first in very slow and converted of ____ for self and giving the profile. The work was done by night. It was not until the 10th that the work was sufficiently advanced to cover company and that day work. The 5th & 6th battalions worked on an MG pill box tiffin away [illegible] camouflet. Inside dimensions 15 x 8. Well 2' thick Roof 3'-6". The area of new shelters proposed over 10 lys, and they work not day during the [illegible] was that fatiguing parties and using the profit. Progress on the "D" type shelters on the front line on the night of the Brigade Sector was satisfactory. Early in the month Divn & Divnl HQs called to design & here shelters making them stronger. A new of my men and consisted of a flange 5 made (4 hr was over sand bags and the Cements placed on top. The air space between 5'-9" was left. The under roof was supported on a new of pit props also each side—closely packed.	Sketches of these shelters attached.

A4945. Wt. W14422/A1160 350,000 12/16 D.D.&L. Forms/C/2118/14.

WAR DIARY
INTELLIGENCE SUMMARY
(Erase heading not required.)

Army Form C. 2118.

Place	Date	Hour	Summary of Events and Information	Remarks and references to Appendices
CORBIE	1-1-18	6	That particular dawn was decided upon owing to the difficulty of concealing in the front line – the difficulty of getting relief by our infantry place. Ourselves were considerable as the transport of the stores, large quantities of cement etc, was to have carried out very difficult. Even with the form and the transport of stores prevented certain difficulties. Each shelter for Lots 3 men or to be properly covered the camps of about 6 tons required. The total number of shelters undertaken was 60 & of this size. Approx 2 of 6 were amongst the most of the intense shelling of trench and I the enemy shell position but 8 of a large size – due to the size of the shelters total – 11 shelters. It was found possible to carry up all material by hand through the trenches having previously been into B Cap, as of the north 6 and 8 of the shelters were occupied but were not quite finished as they had not got all the necessary covering clicks on them.	
	31-1-18		Then the Kan came in to resume operating were pushed forward. It was on the 9" & 10" of the month that covering was resumed and Right & Left Battalion HQ and the shelter in KING'S ROAD at A.9.9.70.35	

WAR DIARY
INTELLIGENCE SUMMARY.
(Erase heading not required.)

Army Form C. 2118.

Instructions regarding War Diaries and Intelligence Summaries are contained in F. S. Regs., Part II. and the Staff Manual respectively. Title pages will be prepared in manuscript.

Place	Date	Hour	Summary of Events and Information	Remarks and references to Appendices
CORPS	1-1-18		proceeded on a moonlight recce Run Rd of N. of the line presents the better shelter in KINGS ROAD.	
	31-1-18		Offrs – 6, O.R.s 8 men in double bunks. Inside measurements 8' × 8'. Height 5'-6". The roof was designed the 3'-6" Thick — reinforced cement. To start framing the roof, 9 steel rods were laid across and 3 sheets of Rosted Iron laid on them. On the 11" out a new concrete job was started viz:— a shelter for a Power Buggy. A Motor Lorry not near Left Batt HQ. A kind of elephant shelter was used for the job — raised above floor level to increase the head room by this. Inside measurement by this shelter was 7'-6" × 5'-6". Reinforced cement walls 2" thick and roof 3'-6" thick over the crown. It was about the time when the job was started that a few quantity of tar was becoming available for reinforcing and was able to obtain a surfacing as at time first [illegible] in our job by Dor Civil well dayed. As a result it was decided	

WAR DIARY
INTELLIGENCE SUMMARY.
(Erase heading not required.)

Army Form C. 2118.

Place	Date	Hour	Summary of Events and Information	Remarks and references to Appendices
CORBIE	1-1-18		B. was busy in the walls and roof of the Power House Shelter and XPYY in the floor. This made a waterproof job. In the KING'S ROAD shelter	
	31-1-18		water came up in the roof and XPYY in the walls and floor. In the Coy HQ shelter in RICHMOND TRENCH a similar design was decided on. In the shelters at Right + Left Batt. HQ it was decided to continue to use XPYY throughout.	
			With the thaw came trouble with trenches caving in and water often knocking in and the way chiefly afterwards followed by heavy rains the trenches in some places became impassable and the drainage arrangements needed a great deal of attention. The trenches together this went into condition on the 17th & 18th. At & simultaneous with the relief of the 125 Inf. Bde. by the 126 Inf. Bde. An extra company of the 1/4" South Lancs Regt. was allotted to work in the brigade area and they commenced work with 4" mat. finishing on the night of 24/25th. They worked in the right of the sector in the front line and the sap of the communication trenches leading into it [?]. These were the only trenches which were really impassable, others being merely wet.	

Army Form C. 2118.

WAR DIARY
INTELLIGENCE SUMMARY.
(Erase heading not required.)

Instructions regarding War Diaries and Intelligence Summaries are contained in F. S. Regs., Part II. and the Staff Manual respectively. Title pages will be prepared in manuscript.

Place	Date	Hour	Summary of Events and Information	Remarks and references to Appendices
CORBIE	1-1-18	6	The first Bttn. had lives in which not was done was from Beginefter of SCOTTISH TRENCH and YEAR CUT in A9a & the neighbourhood of A 30 in A9d	
	31-1-18		A few days K.O.R. The man worked with new recruit but tools were nearly obsolete & fell. The man for his own part it had been decided to shift again to defended localities in the front line and Brigade did not wish any recruitment was between Ben Walkies, the Being to keep the forward edge and let the earth assume a natural slope. The excavation trenches was on which work was done were BERKELEY STREET in A9a & A9d which has covered in Lanky and THE # AVENUE in A9c and A9d. The little had not caved in but was about 1' deep & thick mud. All the trenches were in possibly condition by Keith the pioneers left the job. On the 9" inst. work was started on excavating No 2 new shelters in HILDA'S REDOUBT A9c 5.3 this work was not carried on	

WAR DIARY
INTELLIGENCE SUMMARY

Army Form C. 2118.

Place	Date	Hour	Summary of Events and Information	Remarks and references to Appendices
GORRE	1-1-18		continuously as labour was not always available. It was rather a standstyle. Progress was considerably hampered by the approach	
	31-1-18		of bad weather. During the wet weather no all excavated had to be carried out in dug-out. The intention was to erect two shelters but the but to type. If required events of reinforced material become available; otherwise a solid floor concrete. The excavation was not finished at the end of the month.	
			Other miscellaneous work undertaken during the month were construction of gravel dug-outs, repairs to water pipe & storage tanks, erection of one new tank in FESTUBERT KEEP, slight alteration to a gun sand store expansion of the embrasure of a new gun pit & light T.M.B. at A.G.C. 66, completion of the concrete shelter in GUNNERS SIDING at A.G.C. 64, and additional work on the 6" T.M. Emplacements at A.G.C.35.25. From the letter it was arranged that the T.M. should provide labour to complete but this has difficulty in finding so that any men were little be spared they were put on this job, the principal work there being to	

WAR DIARY

INTELLIGENCE SUMMARY.
(Erase heading not required.)

Army Form C. 2118.

Instructions regarding War Diaries and Intelligence Summaries are contained in F.S. Regs. Part II. and the Staff Manual respectively. Title pages will be prepared in manuscript.

Place	Date	Hour	Summary of Events and Information	Remarks and references to Appendices
CARRE	1-1-18		Construction of Officers entrance to dugouts	
	6-1-18		In the Crypt workshop at Bgd HQ a considerable number of duckboards were covered with "Wire wearing". It was found that by cutting up rolls into 3 strips, each 1' wide a very satisfactory job could be made of it. Also a large number of small trestles or "stools" were made for dugboards to rest on. 5'6" & the "Baby Elephant" Shelters were made in this workshop also.	
	6-1-18		2/Lt A. WEST returned from course at I Corps Gas School. Report good.	
	6-1-18		2/Lts PENNEY, WHITEHEAD, TURNER & SEALE returned from 1st Course for Junior NCOs at the 42nd Divl Wing. All OC were given a good report during the course.	
	9-1-18		2/Lt SETTLE went sick. 2/Lt DANIELS proceeded on course at I Corps Gas School. Returned 20-1-18 Failed.	
	13-1-18		2/Lts WEST, FORLAND, WILSON proceeded on 2nd course at Divl Wing.	
	10-1-18		Capt CRAIG proceeded on a course in How. & R.L. Tump Line with Canadian Corps. Returned 17-1-18.	
	14-1-18		Lieut J.V. HUGHES proceeded to Veterinary course at N°10 Veterinary Hospital NEUFCHATEL. Course commenced 25-1-18	
	26-1-18		Lieut Louis Frit Mahilane 6/R Fraised as a churopodist	

WAR DIARY
INTELLIGENCE SUMMARY
(Erase heading not required.)

Army Form C. 2118.

Place	Date	Hour	Summary of Events and Information	Remarks and references to Appendices
GORRE	26-1-18		Lieut J.Y. HUGHES commenced 14 days leave in U.K.	
	27-1-18		Lieut-Col A.N. LANFORD rejoined company from 1 months leave in U.K.	
	29-1-18		9/Cpl CONNOR proceeded on Course at I Corps Gas School.	
	30-1-18		Capt. C.E.T. JONES and Sergt W. HIGGINS proceed on Bridging Course at AIRE	
	31-1-18		Strength of Company	
				Off O.R. H
			Attached 127" Inf/Bde Pioneers – 101 N1
			Bde Workshops – 6 –
			Rams – 1 –
			42 Div Signal Co. – 5 –
			Burial Party – 56 –
			42 Div R.E. Fwk Party
			R.O.D – – –
			4 – 171 – N1
			Details HQ R.E 42nd Div 1 21 –
			Leave to U.K. 1 5 –
			Hospital 1 12 –
			A.E. Course – – –
			Brig Lamp Course 2 38 –
			2 – 345 – 70
			4 212 70
			Ration Strength of Company	

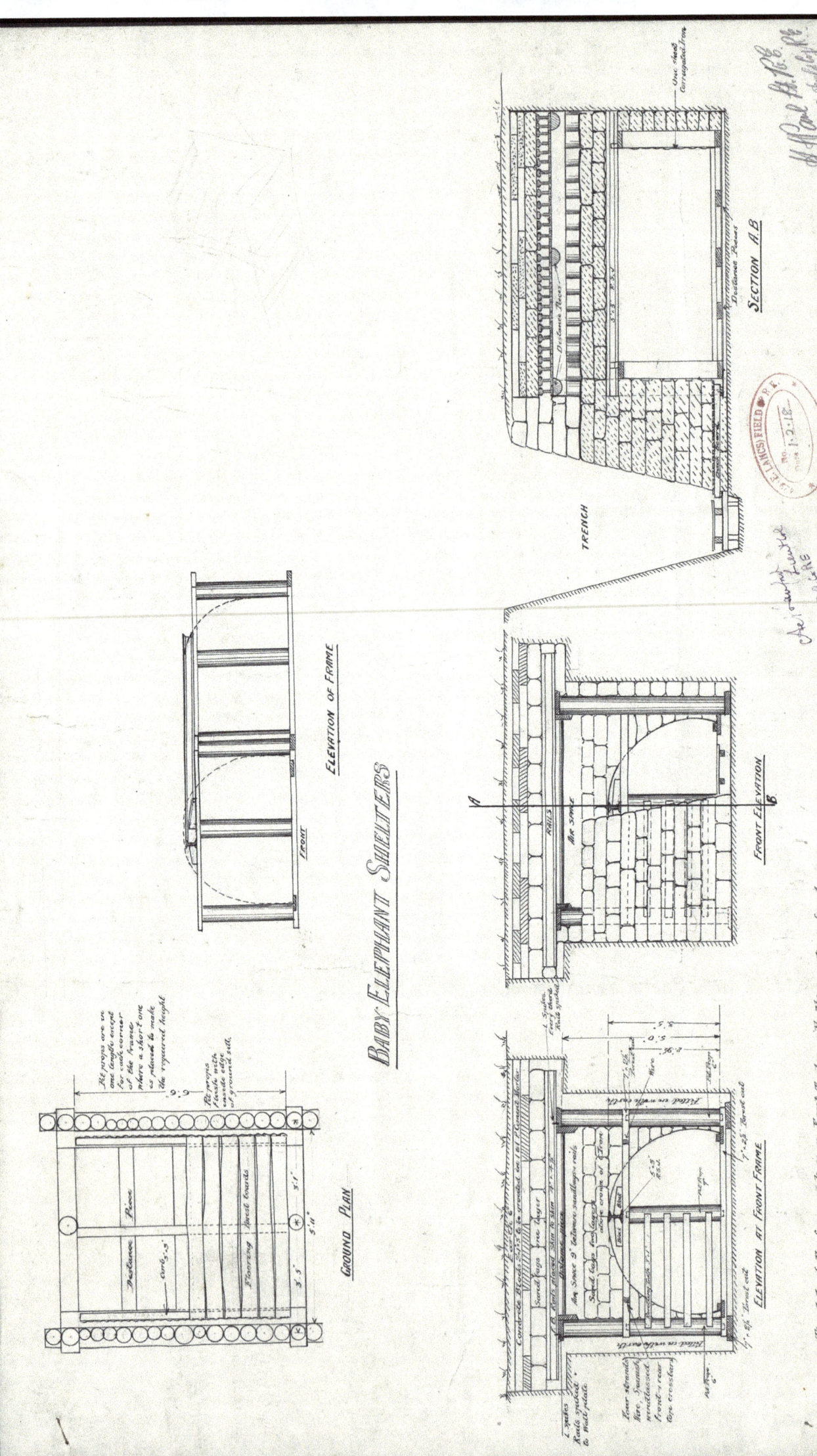

WAR DIARY

INTELLIGENCE SUMMARY.

429th FIELD CO.
R.E.

February 1918

Volume 4

WAR DIARY
or
INTELLIGENCE SUMMARY.
(Erase heading not required)

Army Form C. 2118.

Place	Date	Hour	Summary of Events and Information	Remarks and references to Appendices
CORBIE	1-2-18		Strength of Company	
				O. O.R. H.
			Attached	0 7 212 70
			127 Inf. Bde. Pioneers 4 100	
			Notified	
			42 Div. Sigs. 6	
			Burial Party 1	
			R.E. Park (42 Div) working part 5	
			R.O.D. 56	
			R.A.M.C. Liaison 1	
				4 170
				11 382 70
			Detached	O O.R.
			Leave to U.K. 1 21	
			Hospital 6	
			Mob. RE 42 Div 10	
			Brigading Course MTRE 1 2	
			Gas Course 1	
			Senior N.C.O. Course 42 Div Wksg 3	
			O.R.E. Park 42 Div 3	
			Carpenters Course 1	
			Bde Salvage section (126 Inf Bde) 2	
			2 40 Return	
			Strength 9 342 70	
"	1-2-18		During this period work on left & right Batt. Headworks & MG emplacements	
	6.11.2.18		in Kings Rd. was vigorously carried on & completed although progress was very	
			considerably delayed through lack of cement & delay in delivery of same. Toy	
			the same reason work on Coy. HQrs on Richmond Street had to be abandoned	

Army Form C. 2118.

WAR DIARY
or
INTELLIGENCE SUMMARY.
(Erase heading not required.)

Place	Date	Hour	Summary of Events and Information	Remarks and references to Appendices
GORRE	1-2.11.16			
	11.2.16		The Coy was informed that no cement for the second shelter all right. But this was available the work had therefore to be stopped as no cement was available for this purpose. The whole of the shelter party shelters on the fire line were completed, night parties being worked regularly placing meeting covers of concrete blocks on the roof & camouflaging same with sods. The 6" T.M. emplacements in GUNNERS SIDING were completed as far as R.E. work was concerned & the guns are in use. It was found from information of the first two designed by the previous company were if anything too rigidly strutted whilst others led to the greatest tiring of the stays done. Arrangement of upper cushions between the plate the platform might obviate this. It is also to be recommended that a heavy block of concrete be placed in position behind the kicking baulk as no arrangement of pile driver into the ground appears to be strong enough to take the recoil. It moves however the position but the ground here was exceedingly soft. A sketch of the suggested alterations to attached.	

A0945. Wt. W11422/M1160 350,000 12/16 D. D. & L. Forms/C./2118/14.

WAR DIARY
INTELLIGENCE SUMMARY.

(Erase heading not required.)

Army Form C. 2118.

Place	Date	Hour	Summary of Events and Information	Remarks and references to Appendices
GORLE	1.11.18		On 1/11/18 the 2nd Batt. S. Lanc. Fusiliers returned to their unit there mentioned was left in the hands of the battalion in the line of support.	
"	6.11.18		Aint Ruln. order 109 of today recorded the award of the Belgian Croix de Guerre to the undermentioned Officer, N.C.O & men of this Company in recognition of their services whilst the Division was in Belgium. Lt. Col A N LANFORD R.E. 4420 S.S C.S.M J.H CONSILL R.E. 442059 Lt.Qt J ROBINSON (mtd) R.E. 478591 Spr R.J. SPAVEN 4420	
"	16.11.18		2nd Lieut. J.E.H. NICOLSON & C.S.M J.H. CONSILL proceeded on Course of Instruction at 1st Army School of Instruction (Infantry) HARDELOT. Lt. J.V. HUGHES returned from duty to U.K. & Course of Instruction in Veterinary studies at No 13 Base Veterinary Hospital NEUCHATEL	
"	11.X.18		The veterinary Officer, N.C.O's and men took part in conjunction with a party of the 19th Battn the Manchester Regt in a raid on enemy lines as recorded in attached narrative of the Operations.	
			2nd Lieut D. C. CHAPMAN, 107587 L/Cpl N. COLLINS, A/42233 Spr J.T.M°CARTHY 486546 Spr R.C. WILLIAMS, 44473 Spr T.H. JOHNSON, 37500 Spr W.G. TUDOR 442233 Spr J FIELDING and 400446 Spr J. MACHIN	

WAR DIARY
or
INTELLIGENCE SUMMARY.
(Erase heading not required.)

Army Form C. 2118.

Place	Date	Hour	Summary of Events and Information	Remarks and references to Appendices
GORRE	11/2/18		4 Officers & 100 OR of attached infantry supplied by the 5th M.G. Coy 98th	A.J.P
			Machineted returned to their units prior to move	
"	12/2/18		Lieut H.T. PAUL proceeded on 14 days leave to UK	A.J.P
"	13/2/18	10pm	Coy left GORRE	
LES HARISOIRS (Commune du Mont Bernenchon near ST VENANT)	"	4am	Arrived	A.J.P
	14/2/18		Captain C.E. TURNER, Lieut JONES (and Sergt W. HIGGINS) proceeded from 1st Army Bridging School, AIRE after 14 days course of Heavy Bridging. Not on stated in war [...] taken over from 419 Field Coy R.E. 55 Div. This consisted of a large amount of work near the villages of LESTREM, ZELOBES and LOCON via LOCAN - Rue de Marais - 8 Rue Delannoy. All the Bridges are all of the BETHUNE - LOCON - LESTREM road. They were in all cases supported in three crossings	
	15-2-18		rays with forelarer & M.G. Coy takng them. Work on the wings defenses were started & up out of 9 faults	A.J.P
	19-2-18		On the 16th inst the 1/5 East Lancs Regt began work on the way under the Coy after which the work was undertaken as &	A.J.P

WAR DIARY
or
INTELLIGENCE SUMMARY.
(Erase heading not required.)

Army Form C. 2118.

Place	Date	Hour	Summary of Events and Information	Remarks and references to Appendices
LES HARISOIRS	15-2-18		Lorries were used to convey the men to the work. On the 19th no work was	
LES HARISOIRS	19-2-18		started & the section of a YMCA hut at LECKEME 1.3.C.9.4	
LES HARISOIRS	20.2.18		Company moved to HINGES. The weather being very wet & cold, it was decided as far as possible that the men would be HINGES billets and move from there to	
HINGES			work.	
HINGES	21-2-18		The unit at local [illegible] its war establishment on the 26th July. In addition men were [illegible] and stated at 655/45 on the 24th not [illegible]	
	28-2-18		CRE 46 Div. [illegible] 26th and [illegible] 26th [illegible] was a [illegible] as a [illegible] for [illegible]	
			[illegible] AISNE — [illegible] and the [illegible] [illegible] of 3 [illegible] [illegible] 11 [illegible] was taken on the 26 & 27 and 8th [illegible] 419 [illegible] 55-Dn on the 28th It was arranged to take in Hd the 422 and 423 [illegible] 53-Dn on the 1st and 2nd March. The [illegible] [illegible] [illegible] to the building. 1.3 [illegible] was broken [illegible] the [illegible] 65th Div. and the [illegible] [illegible] and the [illegible] to the [illegible] in the [illegible] along the [illegible]	

WAR DIARY
or
INTELLIGENCE SUMMARY.

(Erase heading not required.)

Army Form C. 2118.

Place	Date	Hour	Summary of Events and Information	Remarks and references to Appendices
LES HARISONS	16-2-18		442016 Sgt W. GRAY, 442022 Cpl R. OGILTMORE, 442322 2/Cpl F. MOLE & ser N.C.O. Senior	
			and 342647 2/Cpl W.B. NORRIS, 477036 Spr W. JENKINSON to junior N.C.O. Senior at	
			42nd Divl. Wing	
	18-2-16		L/Cpl CRAIG to Messrs Bridging Course at 1st Army Bridging School	
	19-2-18		2/Cpl WOOD. H. & Spl. SEALE to 2/Cpl MOAT, L/Spl MARTIN, Sapper MACHIN to Lewis Gun Course unit	
			1/5" Manchester Regt. L/Cpl WOOD went on to 1/5" Lewis Gun on 27-2-18 with a	
			to Inventing Rate to Cpts Lewis Gun School.	
HINGES	21-2-18		2/Cpl CUNNINGHAM to 1st Corps Gas School for working gas course	
GORAB	1-2-18		2/Cpl CONNOR to 1st Corps Gas School for working gas course	
HINGES	24-2-18		2/Cpl WEST to 1st Corps Workshop School	
	20-2-18		2/Cpl HULME to 19" Fd. Vet. Section for course of instruction signals duties	
LES HARISONS	27-2-18		2nd Lt N. HOLT & 19" Northumberland Fusiliers reports for attached for instruction	
HINGES	28-2-18		2nd Lt M.J. PAUL reported from Leave	

WAR DIARY
or
INTELLIGENCE SUMMARY.
(Erase heading not required.)

Army Form C. 2118.

Place	Date	Hour	Summary of Events and Information	Remarks and references to Appendices
HINGES	26-4-18		Strength R. Engrs O. ORs	
			Attached 7 213 44	
			R.A.M.C. 1	
			127 Inf Bde Workshop 6	
			42 Div Signals 1	
			42 Divl Motor Lorries 1 9	
			8 222 44	
			Detached H.Q. RE 42 Divn 2	
			Leaving 3	
			Hospital 1	
			Courses 1 21	
			1 21	
			Return Strength 7 201 44	
				JM Crawford
				Lieut Col
				O.C. 427 Fd Coy R.E.

Narrative of Raid carried out by 1/9th Manchesters and party of 429 Field Coy RE

Strengths of parties. 1/9th Manchesters 3 officers 96 OR
429th Field Coy RE. 1 " 7 "

Copy of 126th Bde Order No 84
Secret   Copy No 7

126th Infty Bde Order No 84

Ref Sheet 36c NW1
36 SW3 & VIOLAINES No 4 1/10,000   Feby 8/1918

(1) The 1/9th Manchester Regt will carry out a raid on the 16th inst upon the enemy front and support lines in A.3d.

(2) The boundaries of the objective will be
  (a) CT running from A3d 5.5 65 (Front Line) to A3d 61 75 (Support line)
  (b) "   "   "   A3d 47 87 ("   ")   A3d 55 85 ("   ")

(3) The raiding party will consist of 1 Company of Infantry and will be accompanied by 1 officer, 1 NCO & 6 Sappers of 429th Field Coy RE for demolition purposes.

(4) Prior to Z day, in addition to the gaps at the flanks of the objective, the artillery will cut gaps in the enemy wire at the following places
  S28a 85 95, S28a 83 80, S28c 20 80, S28c 02 62
  A3b 40.60, A3b 38.53, and 2 gaps between GIVENCHY and the Canal

  Battalions holding the line will arrange to bring fire to bear upon these gaps to prevent their being repaired.

(5) At ZERO minus 10, two batteries RFA will open at an intense rate upon the enemy trenches opposite Canadian Orchard, where wire has been cut. This barrage will lift at Zero on the enemy support line at this point, and will then die down, ceasing at Zero plus 5 minutes.

(6) At Zero, 6 18-pounder batteries will open upon the enemy front and support lines between A3d 63.20 and A3b 38 40
  Two batteries 4.5" howitzers, 9 6.3 howitzers, Stokes mortars and 6" Newtons will fire on selected trenches, trench junctions, and targets in rear
  At Zero plus 3 minutes the barrage will lift off the objective and a box barrage will be formed along the line, A3d 61.45 - A3d 91 87 - A3b 91 00 - A3b 65 30 - A3b 62 - A3b 38 06
  This box barrage will continue until Zero plus 30 when it will cease

(7) The original barrage on the enemy front and support

Order No 84 (Cont'd)

lines of the objective will be repeated, as soon as notification has been received that the raiding party is back in its trenches, and again at Zero plus 1 hour 15 minutes, with a view to inflicting loss upon any parties of Germans who have re-entered the evacuated trenches.

(8) 126th Machine Gun Coy. and 126th LTM Battery will each have one gun located in New Rose Trench prepared to silence any machine guns which may open fire in the enemy front system between A.3.d.6.20. and A.9.b.70.65.

(9) The raiding party will enter the enemy trenches as soon as the barrage lifts at Zero plus 3 minutes and will commence to withdraw at Zero plus 20.

(10) An Officer of the Brigade Staff will visit the Hdqtrs of units and formations to synchronise watches in the following order, commencing 2.0pm 10th inst, 84th Brigade RFA, 126th LTM Battery, 1/9th Manchester Regt., 126th Machine Gun Coy.

(11) Zero hour will be notified later.

(12) Please acknowledge on attached slip.

(Sgd) B Sanderson
Captain
Bde Major
126th Infty Bde.

Issued by D.R. at 8.0am 9/2/18.

Copy of Addendum No 1 to 126th Bde Order No 84

Secret.
Copy No 7

Addendum No 1 to 126th Infty Bde Order No 84

Feby 10th 1918.

(1) The operation referred to in 126th Infantry Brigade Order No 84 is postponed until 11th inst.

(2) Please acknowledge.

(Sgd) B Sanderson
Captain
Bde Major
126th Infty Bde.

Issued by D.R. at 12 noon.

Copy of letter from OC 429th Field Coy RE to OC RE Party 11.2.18.

Lieut Chapman.

(1) You will take 1 NCO & 6 Sappers in a raid by 1/9th Lprs.
(2) OC Raid is Capt Stevenson 1/9th Manchester Regt.
(3) Your role is to destroy dug outs and trench mortars. OC Raid will indicate to you what is to be destroyed.
(4) Guncotton charges will be made up 20 lbs each in crates with primers etc in each end.
(5) All boxes of Guncotton, fuze, detonators, nobel lightin etc will be tested before any material from them is used.
(6) Any material that you want in the company is at your disposal
(7) You must ascertain what date this will take place also rendezvous and passwords.
(8) All flashes, identification discs, letters, sketches, shoulder titles or anything including field dressing which have any marks or which give away the unit or division must be left behind. Special Identification discs have been issued to you.
(9) New revolver ammunition is on my table for your use, 12 rounds per man.

(Sgd) A.H. Lawford
Lt Col.

Copy of Addendum No 2 to 126th Infty Bde Order No 84

Secret

Addendum No 2 to 126th Infty Bde Order No 84.   Copy No 7

Feby 11th 1918.

(1) Reference 126th Infantry Brigade Orders No 84 dated Feby 8th 1918, Para 11.

Zero hour will be 6.15 pm today.

(2) Please acknowledge by wire.

(Sgd) W Gorrell
Lieut
for Captain
Bde Major
126 Infty Bde

Issued by S.D.R. at 10.0 am.

Memo Re Strength, Equipment and Work of R.E. party engaged on Raid

Strength 1 Officer, 1 NCO, 6 Sappers.

Arms
Officer. Belt, Revolver, Wirecutters and 12 rounds of Ammunition.
NCO. Belt, Bayonet, Wirecutters, Revolver, 12 rounds of Ammunition and Mobile Charge.
Sappers. Belt, Bayonet, Revolver, 12 rounds of Ammunition and Mobile Charge.

Mobile Charges
The charges consisted of light wooden crates containing 20 lbs of Guncotton each with Primer, Detonator and 16 feet of safety fuse at either end.
Nobel Lighters were carried by all.

Work of R.E. Party
Three dugouts were discovered and charges placed and successfully exploded against them. 6 Germans were discovered in one dugout and were disposed of.
The party returned without casualties.

Rehersals
The raid was practiced several times both by daylight and by night against dummy trenches.

Notes on the Mobile Charges
New mobile charges were specially drawn from CE 1st Corps for the purpose of this raid but on testing two of these they failed to explode. The reason was found to be that the ammonal primer down the centre of the charge had no ammonal in it.
Accordingly the provided instructions supplied with these charges was that a detonator should be placed through the plug provided into the centre of the charge. The detonator being connected by safety fuse to the firing igniter.

and the charge would then be ready for use. What happened in practice was the safety fuse burnt through and the detonator went off in the otherwise empty centre compartment of the charge and failed to explode the charge. Hence it was decided at the last minute to use service explosives which turned out very effective.

Extract from 42nd Divisional Summary of Intelligence No 75.
At 6.15 pm on the 11th the 1/9th Manchester Battn carried out a very successful raid on the enemy front and support lines NE of GIVENCHY between the GT A3 d 53 70, to A3 d 58 76, and GT from A3 d 47 87 to A3 d 55 88. The wire at this point, and as a feint at three other points, had been previously cut by our Artillery and T.M's. The raid was carried out under cover of a box barrage, and Heavy Artillery co-operated by neutralizing certain enemy batteries. Three wounded, and three unwounded prisoners, and one Machine Gun were taken, and heavy casualties inflicted on the enemy, twenty dead being found in their trenches. Our casualties were 1 Officer and 3 OR, all slightly wounded.

Extract from 42nd Divisional Summary of Intelligence No 76
Operations
     The successful raid in A 3 d at 6.15 pm was mentioned in yesterday's summary; casualties inflicted on the enemy in their trenches are now found to be 25 dead, as well as

7 prisoners. In the few hours before the raid, Field Artillery fired 478 rounds chiefly on wire and datum points, and between 6.15 and 7.35 pm other 4,366 rounds were fired as a barrage. M and H TM's fired 147 rounds, L T M's 230 rounds, and MG's 12,000 rounds in support of the raid.

Enemy Operations

Hostile fire during our raid was insignificant and misplaced, only between 5 and 10 rounds from FA falling in vicinity of A.3 central, and a number of rounds TM on Princess Island (A.3.c.), a few rounds Granatenwerfer were also fired at the commencement of the bombardment. Some hostile fire was directed on to vicinity A.16.a.8b., and of A.9 central and front of Division on our left. Hostile MG's in the sector were silent until about 7.10 pm.

During the day Artillery and TM hostile activity was slight and E.A. nil.

Intelligence Flares

About 6.20 pm during our barrage enemy put up numerous white lights all along the front, these burst into two green lights. Enemy continued doing this whilst barrage lasted.

At 6.38 pm when last barrage started, white lights were sent up which burst into two red lights, these continued till firing ceased. There was no apparent result to these signals. Enemy S.O.S. appeared to be green rockets in pairs.

A.W.Bamford Lt. Col.
O.C. 4/9 Field Bgh R.E.

42nd Divisional Engineers

429th FIELD COMPANY R. E.

MARCH 1 9 1 8

Army Form C. 2118.

WAR DIARY
or
INTELLIGENCE SUMMARY.
(Erase heading not required.)

Vol 14

429th FIELD Coy R.E.

MARCH 1918

Volume 4

Army Form C. 2118.

WAR DIARY
or
INTELLIGENCE SUMMARY.
(Erase heading not required.)

Instructions regarding War Diaries and Intelligence Summaries are contained in F. S. Regs., Part II. and the Staff Manual respectively. Title pages will be prepared in manuscript.

Place	Date	Hour	Summary of Events and Information	Remarks and references to Appendices
HINGES	March 1st		No.100512 A/Sjt. CUNNINGHAM from 2nd Corps Gas School. Sappers employed on wiring & digging in at ESSARS and LOCON - LESTREM line & Maintaining Pontoon Bridges.	
			Strength of Coy. at 1/3/16	
			Attached — O.R.	
			7 >13 44	
			R.A.M.C. — 1	
			137 City Co. Workshop — 6	
			41 Divn. Signals — 1	
			47 Northumberland Fus — 1	
			8 >22 44	
			Attached HQ & Bn R.E.	13/13
			Siege	
			Trenches	
			German	1 - 13
			Relative Strength	7 >20 44
	2nd		No.107587 A/Cpl. COLLINS W. } awarded the Military Medal for work connected with rail 37552 Sapper TUDOR W.E. } by 1/9th Manchester Regt on Feb 11th 1916. Sappers on work as above.	
	3rd		had as above.	
	4th		had as above. Lecture by Div. Commander to all officers & men. Two Coys. 1/3rd Monmouth. Batt. att'd.	
	5,6,7th		A/Cpl. account officer on work.	
	8th		had as above.	
	9,10,11th		Work as above. 1st A.R.D. 2489 A/L. 573/16 seconded to Corps on w'd. 7th A.A.0325 2nd Cpl. HULMES.T.	
	12th		Work as above. to Latter duties. 2nd Lt. CHAPMAN D.C. to 1st Corps Gas School.	
			Work as above. Hut now erected on Shore pieces of light Pontoon bridges at VIEILLE CHAPELLE.	

WAR DIARY
or
INTELLIGENCE SUMMARY.
(Erase heading not required.)

Army Form C. 2118.

Instructions regarding War Diaries and Intelligence Summaries are contained in F. S. Regs., Part II. and the Staff Manual respectively. Title pages will be prepared in manuscript.

Place	Date	Hour	Summary of Events and Information	Remarks and references to Appendices
HINGES	Mar 13th	8.0 AM	Huts as 12th	CMR
	14th	10 AM	Left for OBLINGHEM	CMR
OBLINGHEM	14th	12.30 PM	Coy arrived & billeted. Huts provided in other bays & bridge at VIEUX CHAPPELLE	CMR
	15th	8.0 AM	Huts & hindrances & maintenance of bridges continuing. B/Para/H 12·6 Gd. Addresses lined that all lyds	CMR
	16		2/Lt BUTTERTON & B CoS & 2/Lt. HOLT & 40 CoS. B.H. attached from 48th P.E.(Prov.) Pass'y	CMR
	17th		and with orphans to reach OLDHAM. Mentioned on 15th. 4 Inst. Instructor arrived from 15 Bn	
			Coy partly in work remainder in Bayonet fighting musketry instruction - Lewis gun instr	
			Sergt GRAY. Cpl BRIGHTMIRE. MOLE 2/Cpl NORRIS Sapper JENKINSON from course at	
			Divl Wing. RE Coy on Pontooning out at Divl Wing. 2/Lt WOOD from 15 CoS to G. School	CMR
	18th	6 AM	Coy employed as above. Plus 8 OR sent to BUR BURE SCHORLS YMCA hut	CMR
	19, 20	8.0 AM	Huts as above	
	21st		No 2 & 3 Section to NOEUX-LES-MINES Found under CE 1st Corps. YMCA hut at LAPUGNY & others	CMR
OBLINGHEM	22nd	8 AM	Coy employed as indicated above	CMR

WAR DIARY or INTELLIGENCE SUMMARY

Army Form C. 2118.

Place	Date	Hour	Summary of Events and Information	Remarks and references to Appendices
OBLINGHEM	22nd March		Erecting YMCA hut at BURBURE. Nos 2 & 3 Sections at NOEUX LES MINES under CE 12 Coy. Remainder of Coy — mainly staying in fatigue Coy.	
	22nd March	9.07	Received order to embus for LABUISSIERE 10.30AM O.23L. Issued order to party in YMCA hut & driver also Nos 2&3 Section. Sent Limbers & receipts for vehicles. Proceeded to make Coy dump at GONNEHEM with 42 DAC as ordered. Left 2 Sappers in charge	
Nuthé	23rd	4.30AM	Nos 2 & 3 Sections returned from NOEUX LES MINES.	
		5.10AM	Party returned from YMCA hut at BURBURE	
		8.17AM	Dismounted personnel bus cyclist left for LABUISSIERE	
		9.17AM	Transport & cyclists left	
		11.25	Arrived LABUISSIERE. Embussed with 12.5 Bde at 11.31AM.	
ADINFER	23	8.13 PM	Detrained & marched to AYETTE	
AYETTE	23	9.30 PM	Arrived & remained in trim	
AYETTE	24		HEarg 9 guns tractors to all day. Anti-gas comm up & dug in in 5,6,7 March ch. Regt close to us at M. aerodrome COURCELLE	
	24	7 PM	Ordered to get ft. full system of defence. No instructions as to which units were to take orders.	
LOG EAST	24	8.15 PM	Arrived FOR EST LODGE. No guides received, present to take unit to St system/ dispositor. March 3 hrs. 12.5 Bde also when flung to Batt. N.Fusiliers (Pioneers). 427C.RE Herevolunt.	
		9.30 PM 9.15	Batty pressed us guns towards COURCELLE. Reported absence of guides to CRE.	
		10.15 PM	Moved 427 & 429 Coys toward GOMIECOURT to try and St defence position. Reported action at CRG	
		11.57 PM	Arrived 2 mile NYACHIET-LE-GRAND. Informed by RA officer enemy about 600yds off. Ordered 427-429 to have	

WAR DIARY
or
INTELLIGENCE SUMMARY.
(Erase heading not required.)

Army Form C. 2118.

Place	Date	Hour	Summary of Events and Information	Remarks and references to Appendices
ACHIET-LE-GRAND	25 March	12.15am	Railway embankment. Regt. Runners left HQ to find out what was happening where the enemy were. Cyclemen on embankment under 2/Lt PAUL & ATKISON. Found B6 SEYMOUR & FARGUS also CRE HQ in château GOMIECOURT. Reported my news and Lieut Glad Staker. Ordered 96 Tww 427-429 Coy (by B6° SEYMOUR) to raid cutting running NNE from A28 B02 (57CNW) to dig in & fight if necessary. Sent him to 4.27-4.29 Coy via station near Major MOUSLEY of HQ & then on the railway cutting.	OAM
A28 B02 (57CNW)(200E)	25 March	1.20am	Found 7o MANCHESTER Regt (many at Rly cutting) my HQ flank, planned attack with 125 Tm & my sept + also 6 MANCHESTER Regt. Relieve 1/40 Div RE Coys cancelled. (by whom C.R.E.?)	OAM
		2.0am	4.27-4.29 G.R.E. arrived sent to 125 Bde HQ for orders. (awaiting C.R.E.co)	CAM
		3.15am	Reported above action to CRE	CAM
		4.20am	Sent orderly 4.27 to Coy runners to 125 Bde	CAM
		10.0am	Schwand Major MOUSLEY to try to find 425 Div RE Coys. Went to 125 Bde where COURCELLES was taken at 3pm.	CAM
		12 noon	where found oc 231 & 222 arranged situation at 3pm. Arrtle Bombardment of railway cutting lasts till 3. of m 2 RAH4 & 2-427 RE	CAM
		2.30pm	Capt JONES to 231st COURCELLES high mound on horse back near Front 2/3 & A R.F. had gun.	CAM
		3.30pm	Received orders to report 127 Bd. way to 125 Bde & associate until 1/27 Bde same at Rummin.	CAM
A28 B02	4.30pm	left A28 B02 road cutting to 1/27 Bde HQ, GOMIECOURT badly shelled by enemy at B.6h(1) guns.	CAM
LOG EAST WOOD	5.15pm	2/Lt EVANS wounded in Leg by splinter. 2nd Lt Pvt Capt. Nov F30 A9 55 (57CNE) + wounded both to 127 Bde HQ.	CAM
	6.30pm	Found 6th MANCHESTER Regt transport. Learn Bde Staff Capt about COURCELLES Adv Bde HQ near ACHIET-LE-GRAND.	CAM
LOG EAST WOOD	25th	7.0pm	2/Lt NICOLSON & Self & 127 Adv HQ. Found same 10pm about same road near GHQ (57CNW)	OAM

Army Form C. 2118.

WAR DIARY
or
INTELLIGENCE SUMMARY.
(Erase heading not required.)

Instructions regarding War Diaries and Intelligence Summaries are contained in F. S. Regs., Part II. and the Staff Manual respectively. Title pages will be prepared in manuscript.

Place	Date	Hour	Summary of Events and Information	Remarks and references to Appendices
LOG EAST WOOD	25th March	1 p.m.	Told 96 leave Coy when others of regt, as Bde HQ Coy, took aero place	AHH
		11 p.m.	Billet of Coy Billet. M.G. hie arranges HQ EAST – ACHIET. LE GRAND road.	AHH
	26=	6.30 am	Bde ordered Coy to move over to ESSARTS F19(57DNE) & hrs 427G with me, sent this instruct to h 427 G.R.E. no reply. Suffer falling long & had received message to 427 GRE and there prisoners as well, bri. listing 96 mates (ABLAINZEVILLE & East of BUCQUOY)	AHH
LOG EAST WOOD ESSARTS	26th	7.10 am	thro' 96 ESSARTS. Coy HQ at E 24 B 81 (57 DNE)	AHH
	26	9.30 am	Arrived Adv HQ in BUCQUOY. Ran HQ in ESSARTS. 125 Bde HQ at ESSARTS	AHH
	26	12 am	Sew Coy Transport moving toward ESSARTS toward HENNESCAMP	AHH
	26	12 nn	Inside MG Coy arrived in Arto.	
	26	2:30	Informed by HUGHESon march until 127 Transport and 42 Div transport under G.C. CLIVE who it leads to 2nd MT ready at G.C. CLIVE	AHH
	26	3:30	Informed 127 Bde that I had not yet any tools as that cash held held moved on make Div arrangement voted for admn.	AHH
	26	2:30	Informed CRE(C) HQ that CRE glad. M.T. received warning order No 2 referred & no 715. Abnormal hrs that 127 Bde self had orathd.	AHH
	26	3 p.	At CHAPMAN also public details of Hqrs HANNESCAMP of CRE's relay post.	AHH
	26	4 p.	427 (AO E+4/7 N.F. Fusilier (Pioneer) Batt Hd Haplincs set 7 hr from me.	AHH
ESSARTS	27	9.15 pm	Adv 127 HQ moved here to ESSARTS. 126 Bde ormed up 427G +4/7 N.F. Pioneer monites	AHH
		12.15 p	returned suffering staff infants Wells line at the...	
		5.0 p	Refused of CRE Quick Transover others as that any was going to try St. Information here personally	AHH

Conveyed by B.G. HENLEY. OC 427 RE & OC 4/7 N.F. Pioneers

Army Form C. 2118.

WAR DIARY
or
INTELLIGENCE SUMMARY.
(Erase heading not required.)

Instructions regarding War Diaries and Intelligence Summaries are contained in F. S. Regs., Part II. and the Staff Manual respectively. Title pages will be prepared in manuscript.

Place	Date	Hour	Summary of Events and Information	Remarks and references to Appendices
ESSARTS	27 Mar	7.0p	1 & 2 Sections left H. at wart 6th Manchester Regt	att
F10 C		8.15p	3 & 4 Sections left H. at wart 5th Manchester Regt	att
57D NE		9.0p	N. P.S.O. + G.S.96 & TC 127 does not omit 2nd Manchester suffer parties already at work	att
		9.55p	& O.C. 127 Bde does not omit by reserve Regt at all to be drawn from HMN RES CAMP	att
ESSARTS	28th Mar	AM	Section returned from front line having completed allotation - required 1st class q.q.s	att
		AM	areas kent + infantry existing trenches at costanfeios	att
			Put in Div. Reserve with 427. 4.2 P.C.M.E. + 1/1 N.F. Pioneer Battalion at E.24h (57 D NE)	att
		1.25p	P.S.T. with CRE of this W.M. O.C. 2nd garrison office very insistent	att
		3.0p	Instructed Major General Cutout 4.16 L at night + actual where purple line runs. ESSARTS shelled heavily	att
	29th	12 noon	returned to inform that 2nd bn many casualties of 6.5 battn. Regt E. Lancs at Hill 6.10	att
		4.50p	ordered to GOMMECOURT received A166 re relief	att
		6.1p	W12 DL DE offer details run	att
		10.45	B 6 HENLEY relieved GOMMECOURT how started place at once	att
ESSARTS		11.0p	left GOMMECOURT	att
GOMMECOURT	30th	2.0 AM	settled down in GOMMECOURT in dugouts	
		6.10AM	Self + CSM COWSILL went round the field, L.F. Manchester Battalion. Front from the ball, Hill being fallen earth + repeat instructions. pushed at Ch 127 Bde just in my return 12.45pm	att
		10.35	Found with CRE + instructions until 3 am until 11.5p + 24 points in and & Hill 6.10 m trench 3 & Hill to be	att
			arrived 4.30 left 5.30 right at 6.26 126 Bde as usual. Arranged with S Pratt of I/C 126 Bde 9.1 AM + 31st Aug that this service	att
		10.3p	arrived atty. Relief front 127 Bde bof all cary not anothers. Detailed L/T EASTWOOD + party to Infanterie Werkmann ATM	att
			of summer materials	
GOMMECOURT	31	6.30 AM	Approx. EASTWOOD returned having made all night htm transport handed	att

Army Form C. 2118.

WAR DIARY
or
INTELLIGENCE SUMMARY.
(Erase heading not required.)

Instructions regarding War Diaries and Intelligence Summaries are contained in F. S. Regs., Part II. and the Staff Manual respectively. Title pages will be prepared in manuscript.

Place	Date	Hour	Summary of Events and Information	Remarks and references to Appendices
ESSARTS	March 31	9.0am	Reported to G.O.C. 12-8 Bde re 2 army pants. Arranged with Staff Captain for new transport to bring material to be brought to ESSARTS. Whilst there the Divl Commander arrived & was shortly afterwards met with other points.	AJL
		12.45	Returned to Coy HQ. Abroad CRE about 12.6 + 12.7 Bde was coy. Later orders had received 12.7 + 12.8 CRE 80x 7ma. Sappers worked morning & night 8mi intro put as night out the nm indicated in para above.	OEMT

Strength of Coy
Marched
12.7 troops Bde workshop
4 Point Sigs
½ manoeuvration

Attached RE 3 4x2M
                  hors & mt.
Hospitals
Veterinary Corps
ARMC. Transport

Strength in with Coy

	O	OR.	H
	0	1	
		6	
		1	
		4	
	7	3	60
		3	
		m	
	7	197	68
		1x	
	7	218	68

[signatures] H.R.G CRE
W.G CRE

42nd Div.
IV.Corps.

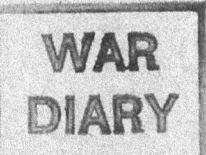

429th FIELD COMPANY, R.E.

APRIL

1918

Army Form C. 2118.

WAR DIARY
~~INTELLIGENCE SUMMARY.~~
(Erase heading not required.)

429th FIELD Co. R.E.

APRIL–MARCH 1918.

Volume 4.

WAR DIARY / INTELLIGENCE SUMMARY

Army Form C. 2118.

Place	Date	Hour	Summary of Events and Information	Remarks and references to Appendices
E23c64 STDNE (Trench)	April 1st	12.1 p	Took over 127 Bde Hqrs reliving 126 Bde who were relieving 127 Bde. Detailed Capt JONES & 6 O.R. to work under C.R.E.	
		5.0 p	Received ring from 126 Bde via 7o Manchester Regt to go into line Army Dl.	
		7.0 p	Left A.G. Billets & Hqrs to Manchester Regt	
		8.0 p	Jones to Manchester Regt & moved off.	
		10.30 p	Taken new line in front of ABLAINZEVILLE from 23rd Middlesex. All quiet. 1/5 E. Lancs on our right. Trench obstructed with driven in on left. Battalion Hqrs old staff in support line west round the line held by to Manchester Regt & 429 CoE	
	2nd April	11.0		
		6.30 am	heart round line held by to Manchester Regt & 429 C.R.E.	
		8.0 am	Hostile shells of front and support trenches by local B.H.Q.	
		12.0 p		
		12.30	Searching for new B.H.Q. found same at F22 Central	
F22 Central		9.0 p	B.H.Q. moved to F2.2 Central. Sappers digging new trenches in rear of outpost line	
F22 Central	3rd April	2.0 am	Heavy shelling of new B.H.Q. new trenches being dug by 5" 9" shell. In Cambrai Offsv.	
		6.0 pm	Sappers both out drove into C.T. 150 yds in rear of front line, went round & ascertained	

Army Form C. 2118.

WAR DIARY
or
INTELLIGENCE SUMMARY.
(Erase heading not required.)

Instructions regarding War Diaries and Intelligence Summaries are contained in F.S. Regs., Part II. and the Staff Manual respectively. Title pages will be prepared in manuscript.

Place	Date	Hour	Summary of Events and Information	Remarks and references to Appendices
F2 Central	3rd April	9.10am	Enemy refused tram at COURCELETTE. No action to be taken if enemy gives little shelling, intermittent all day.	
		7.15.	Sit. Rep. — 127 Bde C.G. Hq E.23.c.64	
E.23.C.64	4th	2.00pm	Wind calm, rather malignant. 127 Bde relief reports 1.26 Bde	
		7.0pm	Sephia started wing & infmg 13 Purple line also wing - infmg strong points	
E.23.C.64	5th	7.45am	Detached to EASTWOOD march duties under R.E.	
		2.30f	Started small runt purple line defence with B.M. 126 Bde Staffel of Rhine	
		7.30f	Recommended that we here know to continue R.E. (2nd 3rd section)	
	6th	5.00am	1.2. 4 Sections wing 13 Purple line infmg strong points, N.5. Power wing 2 Purple line	
		9.00am	Saw O.C. 126 Bde re defences. N. of infmg stong points & O.C. 3 SAN ES reliefs up on	
E.23.C.64	7th	5.15pm	Sit. Rep. 126 Bde up position of wiring 13 Purple line, E SSA RTS hilly other details	
			Sephia wiring — 1st Purple line & strong points. Power in 2nd Purple line	
		4.30f	Received orders from O.R.E. to move	
		7.50	Recent burst average from C.E. Helfekuhn. less 46. 185 Coy	
	8th	5.15	Lt. NICOLSON H.Q. O.R.E HENU as advance party.	
		7.30am	Capt. JONES to C.R.E.	
		7.15hf	Q relieved by 461 G.R.E. marched via FONQUEVILLERS & HENU	
		9.15f	Arrived HENU. Transport drew up with company	

WAR DIARY
or
INTELLIGENCE SUMMARY.
(Erase heading not required.)

Army Form C. 2118.

Place	Date	Hour	Summary of Events and Information	Remarks and references to Appendices
HENU	9-4-18		Resting, bathing, refitting etc.	
	10-4-18			
	11-4-18		Company was inspected together with 125 Inf Bde, 128 H.Q. R.E. and 12 Div. Sig. Co. at 7h5 by Maj. Gen. Cmdg. 42 Div.	
		12.30 pm	Received orders to move 3 sections to SOUILLY - FLOOD Engr. B.S.O., SAILLY-au-BOIS and "CHATEAU de la HAIE SUISSE" at J.16.d.9.6 Sheet 57.? for work in defence lines	
		9.30 am	Capt Jones, Lieut Phil. Nicolson Symonds and Capt. Knox Gymnion and portion of HQ from refitting at HENU Total strength 1/3 old ratio. Proved at 10 am. Coy HQ remained	
	13-4-18		Sappers and 2 Coys. posted with O.C. Chateau de la Haye Suisse, Casemate. The past allotted to R Company was H/11.30 p/m working materials. Returning at 11.30 p/m Rest for every morning attack. No result.	
	14-4-18		Work continued. 126 Bde HQ established in camp suffered some slight damage. By HQ at HENU	
	15-4-18		Work continued. Orders issued that all our Infantry 153 H.Q. and the 2 Bn. in 16' as Standing O.C. 2 Officer and 8 NCOs went to HQ 153 and 16' nights and H.Q. O.C. with to Field over. Later nearer orders to take over 152 H.Q. with 2 Officer and NCOs to General staff of HQ. HA - SAILLY-au-BOIS as arranged. Chateau de la Haie Suisse to Then HA - SAILLY-au-BOIS as arranged. Other officers went to bet. Chateau & in to this suisse to remain morning 57 Div. party detail in mr. O.R.E. Did so.	
HENU	16-4-18		Team Section something by the herman aft. behind our reach of the H section, Lieut detailed to work with Eng. Fd. detailed 3D infell in charge. Lieut Eastwood trained by OC for duties in Division Water Office from Cp. HQ and 14 mention from Cignies and (Cigues) arr'd at SAILLY-au-BOIS.	
SAILLY-au-BOIS			Coy. HQ established at SAILLY-au-BOIS. Trump huts round HQ lane near COIGNEUX	

WAR DIARY
or
INTELLIGENCE SUMMARY.
(Erase heading not required.)

Army Form C. 2118.

Place	Date	Hour	Summary of Events and Information	Remarks and references to Appendices
SOUTY-au-BOIS	17-4-18		Bn. started on digging and wiring defenses from Fellencourt to 152 Bde. Front. Bn. H.Q. H'ts.	appx
			party supplied by 1/6th Bn. Manch'r.	
MEAULTE	18-4-18		Relief of Staff Instructors at B. Coy. 1/7 N.F. Form details to work out the arty. of 127 Bde 6 stops per Bn.	appx
			MEAULTE were ordered to work and were ordered on the morning of the 18th. There were 3	
			N.C.O.s and a 10 stretcher to take the men there and 6 to 125 Bde.	
MEAULTE	19-4-18	8.0.A.	Bn. stayed in B. other 3 stretcher parties. Relays were kept on then stretchers	appx
			and party in making R.O.D. and a small Brach cut by C.O.P. who was Bn.	
			started on improving the "MEAULTE Switch" was put in the village	
			Both strong points and making up 2 guns Leys Cherts, 6 Sellos, 13 small	
	20-4-18	8.0.A.	Bn. carried on a 5 strong points, the remains as developed on a repairing and	appx
			strong pt. and 68 containers full. These as were tells. 16 N.A. Posts of resistance	
			Bn. H.Q. started work on Cherry Ln. B. Coy. to improve the his bn.	
			the MEAULTE Switch Line. 4 Cpl. of the Bn. wereheld to the one	
			started at EDEN ½ N.F. Posters about 1 Br. and it out about 15 Platoon to	
			Bn. continued as above. Proposed to hand over to New Zealand Division	
	21-4-18		Reconnaiss. of front about to Elephant Shelter were Civilian at O.P. H.Q's	appx
	22-4-18		to approach a battalion 127 Bde was to move as newly Coy 2 Cysts	
			in line, and as Battalion to be inserted at the av. on the N.Z. Bn.	
			was O.C. 1/7 N.Z. Bde. Went inco reserve.	
	23-4-18	7.0.a.m.	Bn. started on carrying of Jellicoe and Clinton at O.P. H.Q. Carried on day	appx
			and night in shifts of two and four 1.0.p. — 7.0.p. — 7.0.p. — 10 aan.	
			8 hour Father Clair 6 a 48 hour.	

WAR DIARY
or
INTELLIGENCE SUMMARY.
(Erase heading not required.)

Army Form C. 2118.

Place	Date	Hour	Summary of Events and Information	Remarks and references to Appendices
SULLY-en-BOIS	23-4-18	6 pm	SULLY was shelled. 2/Lt PENNET & 2/Lt MALONE wounded by shell. No. 1 with letter.	
	24-4-18		Shot fills up the next day. No 2. L.G. shot to bits on MERVIENNE Defences that A. 2/Lt Ballen continued to harass wiring by handcarrying to handcarts work and to get the completed.	
	25-4-18		Coy moved to the shoot lines near COIGNEUX. Light casualties attempted. No 3 water details to go 4/27 Goth Bdr. Spot the night in an old time. B Coy had 13 B.S.6 No meeting and 2nd R.F.M. under Rue. MAJOR M. No 3 water moved to Coffin to be encamped. Very fine day. Dr. Q fast got Kempt him and is on By all your men anxious time job having a good shy. No 2 water moved from Sully to him having completed work in the letter.	
COIGNEUX 13 B.S.6	26-4-18		at CAPITOM de la ROSE.	
	27-4-18		By 2/Lt JONES made to SAILLY to take him, leaving right at 4 at SAILLY. Not up B.E.F THUNKLOCKER FOR DUVILLERS	
	28-4-18		and 2/Lt Parker. 143 4, at SAILLY.	
	29-4-18		and MERVIENNE carried in by Gen. Trench Con. And to be moved about 150 to move at 6 to way T a Rifle refgt. All available men up by order	
	30-4-18		Lewis Off. Mr LAWFORD required notify B.E.F. Cpt. to we Cpt. to set of dutie an one to Cpt. Trench, and Change on Ed. Supply to Cpt. PERSONS. Preparation made ready to leave	

WAR DIARY
INTELLIGENCE SUMMARY.
(Erase heading not required.)

Army Form C. 2118.

Place	Date	Hour	Summary of Events and Information	Remarks and references to Appendices
BUSNES 3156	30.4.18		Strength of Company OR Attached R A M C — 5 1/7 Ban Worcester — 1 4/5 R Lin 911 — 1 1/7 N.F (Pm.Bat) 9 — 1 $\frac{O-R \quad H}{7 \quad 701 \quad 73}$ Detached 42nd D.A.C — 20 H.Q 42 DivRE — 8 Hospital — 1 42 D/H.Q — 1 the have lost — 1 $\begin{array}{c} O-R \quad H \\ 1 \\ 8 \quad 209 \quad 73 \end{array}$ Ration Strength $\frac{30 \quad 1}{8 \quad 149 \quad 72}$	

O.C 429 Fd Coy RE
3/5/18

WAR DIARY
or
INTELLIGENCE SUMMARY.

Vol. 16

Army Form C. 2118.

429th FIELD Co R.E.

MAY 1918

Volume 4

WAR DIARY or INTELLIGENCE SUMMARY

Army Form C. 2118.

57 D ?
57 D N.E.

Ref Map 1/40000 1/20000

Place	Date	Hour	Summary of Events and Information	Remarks and references to Appendices
COIGNEUX 13.2.5.6	1-5-18		Strength of Company. See 30th April. Lieut Col A.N. LAWFORD and Batman left the Company to XV Corps. Lieut. Col. LAWFORD took the C.R.E. XV Corps Troops. Company taken over temporarily by Capt. C.E.T. JONES. Works in hand. BEER TRENCH. Defences between FONQUEVILLERS and HEBUTERNE. New posts were sited before a supper line, these being	OBEY
	2-5-18		No 2 section (2nd Lieut NIELSON) relieved No 4 section (2nd Lieut POPE) at SAILLY-au-BOIS. Work started on supporting posts BEER TRENCH. Major J.G. RIDDICK appointed to command the company to rank of temp. 6 126 2/126. Heavy heavy rain receved. Impossible relief on the 6" ult. O.C. went round C/C.	OBEY
	3-5-18		O.C. 502 Coy R.E. (57 Div) Ex. to see works on LA'HAIE SWITCH and BATIENCOURT SWITCH and to show O.C. 502 Coy the works on BEER TRENCH. Divisional Commander also visited the works at BEER TRENCH and made certain alterations to the scheme, embodying a line ??? into a platoon post and adding a empty new Platoon post. O.C. then inspected J. 7 front line posts B.B.1, B.B.2 and 6 supports posts B.B.1, B.B.2 ... B.B.3 6 in L.	OBEY
	4-5-18		B1, B1a, B2, B3, B6 of K3 C.A.2 an intermediate post. At Mt. HEBUTERNE and (B1 L) 2F K3 C.A.2 6 O.R. of 502 Coy R.E. were attached to 502 C. to take over works and 4 O.R. were sent to 502 C.	OBEY

WAR DIARY
INTELLIGENCE SUMMARY

Army Form C. 2118.

Place	Date	Hour	Summary of Events and Information	Remarks and references to Appendices
COIGNEUX	4-5-18		Fine. Men woke and camp. Meanwhile work carried on as usual.	Copy
J.3 & 5.6	5-5-18		Lieut. PAUL & CHAPMAN visited 502 O.B.Co's work on PURPLE (ANZAC) SWITCH and BAYENCOURT SWITCH with a view to starting work on 7th mly if necessary.	Copy
	6-5-18		Whole work entered during the day. 2nd Lieut STEMAN, company no. 5 COUIN Extn. our Camp A. 502 O.B.P.C. in the woods behind COUIN Chateau. Battalion No. 1 & 2 before same run from 50141 an BUS and No.3 water returned from H.Q. and camp for all taken in the new camp.	Copy
COUIN J.1 & 8.4	7-5-18 to 10-5-18		3 melee (N° 1 and 2) on training — drill musketry bayonet drill gas drill etc. Coy. also had baths during this period. Work was carried forward on PURPLE (ANZAC) and BAYENCOURT SWITCHES, working at work ready for infantry working parties to start work on 11th inst. On 8th inst. O.R.E. & S.D.R.E. 72nd Bde. came over BAYENCOURT SWITCH and roughly acted reserve line of PURPLE SWITCH. The latter was roughly planned early morning of 10th inst. for B.G.G.S. Coy. G.S.S. when required. Not was also taken over on a Kamels by Lieut. COUIN at J1C 35.90 on 8th inst as work proceeded on 8" g + 10" nets afterwards it was handed over to 427 Co. R.E. On 9th inst. Revetting division carried out a practice manning of battle position.	Copy

WAR DIARY
or
INTELLIGENCE SUMMARY.

(Erase heading not required.)

Army Form C. 2118.

Place	Date	Hour	Summary of Events and Information	Remarks and references to Appendices
COLIN J.1.6.4.	11/5/18		Working Parties started work on PURPLE (SWITCH) and BAYENCOURT SWITCHES. Total 8 Sections employed. Complying with - 3 on the former and 2 on the latter. Work in Battalion area completed for time being. PURPLE switch and making traverses for... ...in front of and at BAYENCOURT switch, wiring front line and digging supporting posts.	(App)
	12/5/18 to 14/5/18		All Coys work continued. On 13th inst. orders were received to push on with the BAYENCOURT...switches...making 3 continuous...on the PURPLE and BAYENCOURT switches. On 14th inst. orders were received that no metal was to be fixed at present. 427 Coy for work on Knolls by 1 & No 2 section was detached and these worked with O.O.8427 Coy. Lieut NICOLSON went with those was taking charge on this date & later employ...	(App)
	15/5/18		Preliminary working parties were changed on this date to 2nd...began work. Coy put on to BAYENCOURT switch with 3 R.E. sections and no 2 under O.C. 427 Field Coy R.E.	(App)
	16/5/18 17/5/18		Work carried on as on 15th inst. It was arranged that this Coy R.E. Lack was to have a day in camp over a 5 day. On this day men were to be employ in camp. Were in the morning and were taken to bathe in afternoon 16.	(App)

WAR DIARY
or
INTELLIGENCE SUMMARY.
(Erase heading not required.)

Army Form C. 2118.

Place	Date	Hour	Summary of Events and Information	Remarks and references to Appendices
COUIN	16-5-18		Not much new activity on this front. Observation posts along the front of the	CBG
J1 B 8 4			PICKLE SWITCH. Ancoxe Company Infantry were forward as working party.	
			B.C. O5 and O.E. II Cop went above ground proper. Reconn'cs for Purple switch	
			made certain alteration.	
	19-5-18		Colonel Chote HQ & Chote. G. Cornish & OP Power Battalion (14" N.F.)	CBG
			Lieut NICOLSON landed and went on dig out to Lieut HALL 426 Bde with a view	
			to locating new dug outs on the following day.	
	20-5-18		CRC of Div and Adm and Reserve the MORRIS visited as attached by my Cops	CBG
			with a view to taking our the emmetation. Lieut CHAPMAN and O O.R. N°3 motor	
			but R.B.A. to cooks and went on the dry to a new H.D 2" Bd. R.A. for attachment	
			Not us started on Saw dugout to MC Crews near Chatin du de "Noue one at	
			D 30 d 7 5 & the other of J 5 d 00 55	
	21-5-18		On section 428 Batt B a litt'd for work & dugouts under the hill by	CBG
			Lieut LORD. 120 Gets Cenis the & one neighbourly Gents Otherwise	
			for coke as usual	
	22-5-18		O.P. 112 Batt M.G.C. subjects evacuate for 2 new dug outs near SAILLY-au-BOIS	CBG

Army Form C. 2118.

WAR DIARY
INTELLIGENCE SUMMARY.
(Erase heading not required.)

Place	Date	Hour	Summary of Events and Information	Remarks and references to Appendices
EQUIN J.18.b.	23.5.18		N.K. K.10 Junction of 45&R or 2 new dug outs at K.7.c. 55.50 and	
		K.13.a. 40.15. Not at all 4 pigments continued from 6.0 a.m. to 10.0 p.m.	
			duty at bombing dugout. 2/Lt. I.M. Lane Lt. from his coy. by charge to	
			3 L/Cpls of 5th Rem. (Regt) and No water working party of 1 infantry	CRE
			coy @ looked work on his day on his dug outs at Elstow W.G. Have	
	24.5.18		Divisional Commander visited Coy went round the works.	CRE
	25.5.18		Not entirely round	CRE
	26.5.18		Head qtrs. K.12. until 1466 D. 252 K. Coy.	
			started from K. prefer of working with the aid carried on Main V.G. A.DDIEK	CRE
			Lt. 126 J. Bn. "D" proceeded E.C.R.E. 148 for temporary duty there	
	27.5.18		Head quarters on same terms as above @ 40½h 11½ 2nd April 225 Families	CRE
	28.5.18		as absorbed for ambulance as Sgt. John Knighton	CRE
	30.5.18		Major General A. Solly Flood C.B.E. D.S.O. presented the medal ribbons to R. Young	
			Col. R. BRIGHTMORE (M.C.) 2/Lt. L.F.R. NICOLSON (M.C.) C.S.M. J.H. COWSILL (Belgium Croix de Guerre)	
			A. SEPHEN (Belgium Croix de Guerre) Sapper N.E. COLLINS (M.M.) Sapper J. BENNETT (M.M.) Sapper	
			A. SEPHEN (Belgium Croix de Guerre) Sapper R.T.R. ANDREW 428th Batt. M.G.C. and 17th M.G.C. Trainers	DRO
			125 Inf. Bd. M.G. Coy. also 17th M.G.C. and men present as a R. guard.	CRE

A0945 Wt W.11422/M1160 350,000 12/16 D. D. & L. Forms/C/2118/14

WAR DIARY
INTELLIGENCE SUMMARY
(Erase heading not required.)

Army Form C. 2118.

Place	Date	Hour	Summary of Events and Information	Remarks and references to Appendices
COUIN	30.5.18		Lieut HUNTON and 1 O.R. proceeded to 6th Feb C.R.E for instructions	
J1.B.6.4			1 O.R. Eng ranks to join 6 Labour coy	
	31.5.18		Major N.C. RIDDICK wired as follows "have made little progress"	
Gouÿ en	8.6.18		2 O.R. Eng NCOs crew at 4th Div Rest Camp fell 18.5.18	
Artois	12.6.18		2 O.R. Eng NCOs crew at 56 Div Rest Camp fell 28.5.18	
	12.5.18		1 O.R. Eng 3rd Army Rest Camp	
	26.5.18		2 O.R. Eng 3rd Army Rest Camp for 14 days	
				O.R. Hors
			Strength of Company	7 197 73
			Attached RAMC for 117,734 5 OR, 432nd Coy 1 OR	2 9 0
			47 N.E.s 10ff 10R 352 Dinwillie C.R.E 10ff 1 O.R.	11 206 73
			At Calais 3 Officers 1 Off 9 O.R. 2 horses	
			3rd Army Rest Camp 2	2 25 2
				9 181 71

Army Form C. 2118.

WAR DIARY
or
INTELLIGENCE SUMMARY.
(Erase heading not required.)

429th FIELD CO

R.E.

JUNE 1918.

Volume 4

WAR DIARY
or
INTELLIGENCE SUMMARY

Army Form C. 2118.

(Erase heading not required.)

Instructions regarding War Diaries and Intelligence Summaries are contained in F. S. Regs., Part II. and the Staff Manual respectively. Title pages will be prepared in manuscript.

Place	Date	Hour	Summary of Events and Information	Remarks and references to Appendices
COUIN	1-6-18		Intended relief of 57 Div by 42 Div cancelled. Advance party returned from 421 Fit & G	
J.L.8.4.	2-6-18		Orders received for relief of N.Z. Div by 42 Div in HEBUTERNE Sector — night 3/4 inst	
	3-6-18		II Corps front. Advance party to 1st Batt & N.Z.E. for two days attachment to our unit in Line.	
			Hot. measures was continued on Bayencourt and La Haie (Rogl) Switches	
			on dug outs for M.G.C. and a Chateau de la Haie strong points.	
	5-6-18		Second advance party of 1st N.Z.E. for two days attachment to first party returned.	
			An officer of 1st N.Z.E. arrived for attachment to 429 F.C.R.E until relief to take over	
	6-6-18		Work carried on all sites at 2.0 p.m	
COUIN	7-6-18		Left at 9.10 am. Small part proceeded in advance to start work on tunnelled dug outs to	
W. ASHULT on			Arrived at 10.45 am. Transport line at J.31.b. Lemans R. Bus-Couvermount Rd.	
(J17c.1.2) -50Y5			Coys as all A. natives in and Stats and shelters at J17c.1.2	
	8-6-18		Not in Lns on pb plan over from N.Z.E. N° 6 dug outs 2 R.A.P	
			and in defences. 127 Inf Bde in line. Left sector 429 F.C.R.E. who was in the	
			Orders of 127 Bde at 1pm. Bde H.Q. in HEBUTERNE at 2.30 pm. J7 coys	
			divided to Couille and Coillie details at FORT HEROD in K.13.6 Kris	

WAR DIARY
or
INTELLIGENCE SUMMARY.
(Erase heading not required.)

Army Form C. 2118.

Place	Date	Hour	Summary of Events and Information	Remarks and references to Appendices
H.Q 3rd NZ Tunnelling Coy 1916	9-6-16		G.O.C. 127 Bde after an enquiry, has now decided that no 6 electrifying defences would be constructed. FORT STEWART in TRO I and FORT HOD K.21.a. Arrangements were made accordingly. O.C. works taken on loan were employing any extra fatigue party off R HEBUTERNE working gement shelter and against gas and a certain amount of road maintenance. September little knowledge of trade in the HEBUTERNE area was also prior lost.	CRE
	10-6-16		Work was started on FORT HERD and FORT STEWART. At all times I was able to place a considerable quantity of digging and wiring men on heat. I was	
	6,14,16,18		also put to employ although for reasonable by means of tunnellers dug with different lathes. Clay chute possible but newly made.	CRE
	15-6-16		125 Bde relieved 127 Bde on the nights of 14/15 June. No orders parties provided on 15th except for tunnelling. The part of the company not engaged in tunnelling had a day's rest. This inspection commenced.	CRE
	16-6-16		Work on two R.A. dugouts at J.24.b.4.5 and J.24.b.6.9 was taken over by 126 Field C. RE.	CRE
	17-6-16		Deep dugout started in FORT HERD at K.13.6.6.9. A Coy 4 NZE starts	CRE

Army Form C. 2118.

WAR DIARY
or
INTELLIGENCE SUMMARY.
(Erase heading not required.)

Instructions regarding War Diaries and Intelligence Summaries are contained in F. S. Regs., Part II. and the Staff Manual respectively. Title pages will be prepared in manuscript.

Place	Date	Hour	Summary of Events and Information	Remarks and references to Appendices
W.J SMLY 1/2c1/2	17-6-18		Work for 41st M.Brigade under the jurisdiction of Field Coy. Work taken on at FORT HOD and on road maintenance	(App)
	18-6-18		The whole work already referred to work considered as an expenses	(App)
	20-6-18		Have as arranged, had for a C/Troop at C. Small extravers. Installation of C pit in G.G 252 F.M.C & coffee ment points also to 6 until C.F & M.C with dugouts & coffee war put it to and F.C.F of battalion on each work company & enrolment small job apparently called it work. They are exactly this work a full trust remained.	
	21.6.18	3.100 am end of the 3 battalion R.S. Rd came this P.C.F. Troop for 3 days instructions held rim instragement adult are wiped out for a nothing from F. SS 112 Bull No 5 Gross to F, Hill 30 feet only any 30 D flower over to Cal R.C.B Rd & 250. Ft. Le Eglin. One in Dir outto Gme	(App)
	23.6.18		No's attacks for evening instruction returns from crate gone. Length went to 252 Tunnelly Coy attached F.C a short time the ellen Gmyment of attack D.C the F.S Coy in exchange in amount in Tunnelly work.	(App)

A6945 Wt W11422/M1160 350,000 12/16 D. D. & L. Forms/C/2118/14.

WAR DIARY
INTELLIGENCE SUMMARY

Army Form C. 2118.

Place	Date	Hour	Summary of Events and Information	Remarks and references to Appendices
N.Z. SAILLY	24.6.18		Work carried on as already worked on by 282nd and Major Riddock went	
Z1 pl 12	25.6.18		6 NCOs Coster CSM duty alarm of Major J H Mouflet DSO	CXY
	27.6.18		Infantry Lewis Gun review report. NZ Division Commander of parts	
			The Co. 2nd demanded that a new dugout HQ for 2nd Inf. Bn be	
			prepared by entering under a funk hole dugout at M.C. 31 and	CXY
			seeking extra overseer on top of funk hole and taking off to hospital	
			Lieut. J.C. Minuson etc. met & hospital	
	29.6.18		O.C. 2nd Felt ? N.Z.E visited front of B sector in Havencourt taken	CXY
			over one of the works e.g. FORT HERALD	
	30.6.18		Strength B Company	
			Attached R.A.M.E. 1, 1/7 NF ?OR, OR 1/25 Tunneling Co 1 OR	0 OR
			428 Inf Coys. 10R, 125 Inf.Bde 5 OR	7 OR
			Detached HQ Aust. RE 8 OR Jan Pin 2 OR	2 13
			Hopkins 1st & 7th Poston Park Albertville 1 OR	9 225
			Captainsbourne 1 OR HQ 117 Bde 1 OR	
			35 T. Co. R.E. 4 OR, 3rd Army Rest Camp 1 OR	1 25
				8 20·0

Major Shenghe?

Army Form C. 2118.

WAR DIARY
or
INTELLIGENCE SUMMARY.
(Erase heading not required.)

Vol 18

429th FIELD COY. R.E.

July 1918

Volume 4.

WAR DIARY or INTELLIGENCE SUMMARY

Army Form C. 2118.

Place	Date	Hour	Summary of Events and Information	Remarks and references to Appendices
W. of SAILLY-au-BOIS J.17.c.1.2	1-7-18		Works in hand. Defended localities FORT HEROD FORT STEWART, FORT HOD in K.13 4.14. K.20, K.21. 3 tunnelled dugouts under construction, 6 cut & cover shelters, erected at J.17.c.4.2, preparations for installation of new huts for new Brigade HQ at J.17.c.4.2. Wiring of SAILLY CATACOMBS. Lighting at in SAILLY CATACOMBS.	CBJ
	2-7-18		Owing to alteration in boundary of divisional sector extensive work ceased at 4.0 p.m. Two tunnelled FORT HEROD and its dugout. SAILLY CATACOMBS as were taken over by N.Z.E. and all work in HEBUTERNE. At 2.55 am, 2-7-18 a shell fell in the camp and killed Sapper HOLLAND and 4 of N°1 section. Wounded Sappers BURSLEM and STEPHENS-KING KERSHAW, ROYLES, and TOMLINSON, all of N°1 section. The above 4 sappers were buried at BERTRANCOURT MILITARY CEMETERY.	CBJ
	3-7-18		Work was started on two company localities FORT CHARLES (extensions to existing work) and FARM POINT in J.30. Part of the wiring of FORT STEWART was done by a class of NCOs from 126 Bn working under 2/Lieut. 429 H.B.G.R.E. for instruction in light wire entanglements.	CBJ
	5-7-18		Work starts on another locality COOKHOUSE POINT in K.19. All wiring done in this area was high wire with the exception of a shot high along COUNTRY TRENCH in J.24.d. K.19.c. where a length of "Spider" wire was tried. Further forward — FORT HOD etc. Low dannels apron were used.	CBJ

Army Form C. 2118.

WAR DIARY
or
INTELLIGENCE SUMMARY
(Erase heading not required.)

Instructions regarding War Diaries and Intelligence Summaries are contained in F. S. Regs., Part II. and the Staff Manual respectively. Title pages will be prepared in manuscript.

Place	Date	Hour	Summary of Events and Information	Remarks and references to Appendices
W. 8 SHELLY-on-BOIS	6-7-18		2/Lieut V.E. EASTWOOD left for leave to U.K. Boat sailing Boulogne 7-7-18	app
	7-7-18 to 10-7-18		Works continued as already mentioned, with the addition of a new "Cat-a-Cruc" Coy HQ at K27 c 70.95 in front. This company right battalion. Material for this was salved from an old dump on the spot. Miscellaneous small jobs — mostly for 126 Bde	app
	10-7-18		Major J.G. RIDDOCK R.E., O.C. 129 Fd Coy R.E. appointed CRE 42 Div with the acting rank of Lieut. Col.	app
	11-7-16		Lieut. J.F.M. NICOLSON M.C. rejoined from hospital (via ROUEN) New work started. New tunnelled dugout for Bde HQ at J17 c 4.2. Work on dugout J17 c 31 completed. A.D.S. dugout started in SAILLY by Royce with a L.O.L R.E. assistance.	app
	12-7-16		New work started. 2nd entrance to dugout for MCE at K15 d 95.05 (14" mat) R.A.P. at K20.20.6 (12" mat) Tunnelled dugout for Coy HQ at K20 e 35.15 (16" mat)	app
	16-7-18		Work completed FORT HOD (14" mat) Coy HQ shelter at K15 d 15.20 (15" mat) Cat-a-Crew shelter in FORT STEWART (15" mat)	app
	17-7-18		Major M.S. HANMER R.E. arrived and took over command of the company	app
	20-7-18		Preparations made to start 3 new tunnelled dugouts in FORBES STREET K16 c 2.3. K21 d 1.6 K21 d 2.2. Latter two postponed. Later owing to intended local operations.	app
			Left for leave to U.K. Boatmaster BOULOGNE 21-7-18 D.C. CHAPMAN	app

2/A645. Wt. W14422/M1160 350000 12/16. D.D. & L. Forms/C/2118/4.

Army Form C. 2118.

WAR DIARY
or
INTELLIGENCE SUMMARY.
(Erase heading not required.)

Instructions regarding War Diaries and Intelligence Summaries are contained in F. S. Regs., Part II. and the Staff Manual respectively. Title pages will be prepared in manuscript.

Place	Date	Hour	Summary of Events and Information	Remarks and references to Appendices
W. of SAILLY-au-BOIS	21-7-18		New Tunnel & dugout started at K15 c 2.3 by Pioneer Company. Work on FORT STEWART ceased.	copy
	22-7-18		Dugout at K20 c 35.15. Roads on to 179 Tunnelling Co. New dugouts starts at K21 d 1.6, K21 d 2.7. Other new work started:- Coy HQ & NCO Cookhouse & Shelters near left Bdd HQ. Sappers withdrawn from operation of digging and	copy
	23-7-18 23-7-18 6		arrival of Greenwood. & Eggyfood reported from Flange. Repairs carried out at main work at Coy HQ K21 c 65.75. On 26-7-18 work on enemy's new Tunnels dug outs.	copy
	26-7-18		Left Batt HQ K14 d 6.6F and at a Coy HQ K21 c 65.75. On 26-7-18 work on Left Bde HQ was handed over to 179 Tunnelling Co.	copy
	28-7-18		In view of proposed relief of 42 Div by 57 Div an officer of 421 F.C. R.E. arrived for attachment for 3 days to meet on had.	copy
	27-7-18		Whilst of 421 F.C.R.E was on with a view to taking on. In the evening however, a message was received cancelling the relief.	copy
	28-7-18 to 31-7-18		Owing to wet weather & tanks in forward area required attention and on night 30/31st a start was made in these places clearing the bottoms of trenches and revetting with about A Company and XPM panels. Camp to shelves. Working parties it was decided to lay on new tunnelled job to Tunnelly Coy and on 300 mt. assignments were made from the J of the forward dug-outs K15 c 2.3 and K21 d 1.6 to be taken over by 179 Tunnelly Co. during the further days of August. Pioneers and sappers as others also employed revetting on damaged unfinished trenches, revetments etc.	copy

WAR DIARY or INTELLIGENCE SUMMARY.

Army Form C. 2118.

Place	Date	Hour	Summary of Events and Information	Remarks and references to Appendices
W.F. SAILLY-au-BOIS	July 1916			
	1/7/16		During the month the following NCO's and men attended courses	
	2/7/16		2/Cpl COLLINS and 2/Cpl WOOD 6 Divisional Course for Junior NCO's MAILLY — duration 4 weeks	
	6/7/16		Sapper LOWDEN Termination of Carbing Course at Third Army School of Cookery	
	7/7/16		Cpl MILE Assembly of RE Course at ROUEN	
	9/7/16 & 29/7/16		Sgt EVANS GS Course at PREVILLES II Corps Gas School	
	19/7/16	6.39 p.m.	L/Cpl FRY - ditto - - ditto -	
	19/7/16	5.29 p.m.	2/Cpl MORRIS Senior Gas Course at MAILLY	
	24/7/16		2/Cpl WHITEHEAD - ditto -	
	28/7/16		Sgt EARLEY 6 Gas Course at II Corps Gas School	
			Leave 2 Officers and 1 OR proceeded on ordinary leave to U.K. during the month 10 R	
			re-engagement leave and 3 OR leave to Paris	
	31-7-16		Strength of Company	
				O. OR
				7 207
			Attached 1 OR RAMC. 1 OR HQ 2nd Div E 1 OR 48 Brigade 1 OR. 3	
			Detached NO HAZEBROUK 9 OR Kantara 1 OR 3 OR 7 204	
			Hospital 5 OR Rest Camp 2 OR NCOs Course 4/Pns 2 OR	
			NS Course Bnd 1 OR LG Course 1 OR Gas Course 2 OR 1 28	
			Leave to Paris 2 OR Purfleet Park Abbeville 1 OR	
			Ration Strength 6 176	

Army Form C. 2118.

WAR DIARY
or
INTELLIGENCE SUMMARY.
(Erase heading not required.)

Vol /9

429th Field Coy.
R.E.
August 1918

Volume 4

Army Form C. 2118.

WAR DIARY
or
~~INTELLIGENCE SUMMARY~~
(Erase heading not required.)

SHEET N° 57NE

Place	Date	Hour	Summary of Events and Information	Remarks and references to Appendices
SAILLY	1/8/18		Work in hand:- Tunnelled dugouts at K21.b.4.6 - K27.6.9 - K21.d.2.2 - J18.b.4.1	
			K15.c.4.3 - Repairing and duckboarding following Kurerkos- HOME AVENUE	MON
			CENTRAL AVENUE - Cut and Cover shelters at T33.b.5/2 - K20.b.1.8 - K27.b.6.9	
—	2/9/18		Work as abt. Capt C.E. Turner - Tunrs Left Bn Coy to Leuterville Base	mon
			Croumnd J.d.4.7. (KL) Field Coy RE vice Major Zulstieh (on leave)	
—	3/8/18		Day off owing to Brigade Relief.	mon
—	4/8/18		Work ceased the following Tunnelled dugouts K15.c.4.3 - K1.6.4.6 - K21.d.2.2	mon
			new shelter started at K20.c.4.1. for RAP.	
—	5/8/18		Work as abt.	mon
—	6/8/18		Work as abt. 2nd Lt Chapman Joined the Coy from leave in the U.K.	mon
—	7/8/18		Work started erecting & duckboarding HORSES TRENCH in FORT ALPHA.	mon
			and NORTHERN AVEN. U.K. - Lieut Michelson left the Coy on leave in U.K.	
—	8/8/18		Work as abt.	mon
—	9/8/18		Work as abt.	mon
—	10/8/18		Work as abt.	mon
—	11/8/18		Work as abm. Relay Post started at K19.b.4.8	mon

Army Form C. 2118.

WAR DIARY
or
INTELLIGENCE SUMMARY.
(Erase heading not required.)

SHEETS 17 DNE.

Instructions regarding War Diaries and Intelligence Summaries are contained in F. S. Regs., Part II. and the Staff Manual respectively. Title pages will be prepared in manuscript.

Place	Date	Hour	Summary of Events and Information	Remarks and references to Appendices
SAILLY	11/8/18		Work as on 11/8/18	map
—"—	12/8/18		— ditto —	map
—"—	13/8/18		— ditto —	map
—"—	15/8/18		All went as on previous job during & beyond retirement beyond SERRE. 1 N.C.O & 2 Sappers sent to each Batt in Brigade to assist pastents to break "Booby Traps". Trek to SERRE cleared up to "H".	map
—"—	18/9/18		All sections put on Arrowing Trenches & working in new TRACK to SERRE and to everywhere it has been heavily travelled dugouts	map
—"—	17/8/18		Program also	map
—"—	18/9/18		—do—	map
—"—	19/8/18		—do— also steady work in TRACK K29.8. K30.5. new 15th Hill at K31.6.4.8 Repaired R. details also	map
—"—	20/8/18		Starts hrs work on TRACK from K29.8 through K29.a.b.d to COIGNEMPS SERRE at K30.C.05. Received 15° Inf/Sch Shoulder fuller No 95. & sent 1 N.C.O & 2 Sappers to assist y/ch 6 Inf. Corps attacking Tranent. Scotch scrubbing dugouts	map

WAR DIARY
INTELLIGENCE SUMMARY
(Erase heading not required.)

Army Form C. 2118.

SHZ K TJONZ 59 C.S.N

Place	Date	Hour	Summary of Events and Information	Remarks and references to Appendices
SAILLY	23/8/18		Troops at drill. Marching by to run forward	MOH
do	23/8/18		- do -	MOH
do	24/8/18		Parties working forward. Supt. Coys attached bn N°24000F 41st BATTN	
LUKE COPSE			N° (Sapper)WH2298 BAILE Y.R & N°. 207259 Sapper CARNELL H. Sapper	MOH
			Carnell H. having been wounded on ch. 24/8/18. T/C Martin Kellam	
			18.22/8/18. Sapper Bailey wounded in ch 22/8/18 - left SAILLY for LUKE	
			COPSE at 2 p.m. travelled via lines from BUS to Camp Sili	
			SAILLY during evening. Battle Reinforcement road reconnaissance	
			party.	
LUKE COPSE	25/8/18		A.M. on roads between PUISIEUX and MIRAUMONT. Evening	MOH
			moves to run forward k MIRAUMONT. Campbell and Kowalsky	
			been stabled at upp from LUKE COPSE.	
MIRAUMONT	26/8/18		Arrived at station after rough journey being held up at cert level crossings	MOH
			owing to having clearing on road. Working on mile roads at	
			MIRAUMONT	
-"-	27/4/18		Troops at drill	MOH
-"-	28/8/18		Troops as above - at Skin orders received K'MONT k M2 (P/S)	MOH

Army Form C. 2118.

WAR DIARY
INTELLIGENCE SUMMARY
(Erase heading not required.)

SHEET 57C S.W.

Place	Date	Hour	Summary of Events and Information	Remarks and references to Appendices
MIRAUMONT	28/8/18		Stated by in readiness from 11th Brigade details for "pursuit" at my leave notice. Order to arm received at 11.35 pm. Coy H.Q. 24 section but not Knapsack lines.	MOH
PYS M2d7.6	29/8/18		At 1.15 am. Coy less transport moved to M2d 5.7. Had reconnaissance of roads in forward area — owing to Brigade moving forward & no decided known Coy transport to T.H.L.O4. Moved at 5 pm — but was unable to get further than LE 15 AR QUE. M11 c 70.45 on account of shell fire — town of Rano not line to M2 d 57 (approx). Heavily shelled during night — 9 O.R. wounds in now positions dugouts. N° 442353 L/C Mort wounded with pneumatic from N° 3rd 13th Sh	MOH
LE BARQUE M11 c 7.5	30/8/18		At 3.30 am received orders to send 1/4 section to report to H/5 Batt Laws to Section to 1/18 Hampshire Regt. N° section to 1/10 Hampshire Regt attached to PM & app'd section to report to 1/8 Hampshire Regt — 1/4 Chapman Hants. divn to 1/18 Hants to Regt. Day being 1/N° 3 section to 1/5 Batt Hants Regt. N°s 1 & 2 sections employed on road over reconnaissance N° 18002 Corpl Furguson wounded. Other wien wounded	MOH

N° At 945. Wt. W14422/M1160. 350,000 12/16 D. D. & L. Forms/C/2118/14.

WAR DIARY

INTELLIGENCE SUMMARY.
(Erase heading not required.)

Army Form C. 2118.

SHEET 57C S.W.

Place	Date	Hour	Summary of Events and Information	Remarks and references to Appendices
LE BARQUE	30/8/18		11 P.m. British attack — No 46235 Sapper Carlin J.M. & No 30484 Spr Needham S.F. killed — No 50844 Spr Crossman R.T. & No 495174 Pte Burden H.H. wounded and evacuated. 3 known men wounded & not both shot & are eventually died.	MOH
—"—	31/8/18		The 117th Bde relieved the 118 J. Bde. "A" Coy became attached to the 117th Bde. Coy had a quiet day. Three Lines at M 7 & 7-6 shelled during the morning & the TANKARD M.T. P's have two (attached for him working) men killed & two horses.	MOH

Major R.E.

Army Form C. 2118.

WAR DIARY
or
INTELLIGENCE SUMMARY.
(Erase heading not required.)

Vol 20

429th Field Coy. R.E.

September 1918.

Volume 4.

WAR DIARY or INTELLIGENCE SUMMARY

Army Form C. 2118.
SHEET 57C

Place	Date	Hour	Summary of Events and Information	Remarks and references to Appendices
LE BARQUE	1/9/18		Reconnaissance of roads & wells conducted. Route examined past 11.27/Bde HQ at a point about 600 yds E of THILLOY. Attacks' companies at BRICKFIELD E. N. of THILLOY expending actions & to be made by 127 Bde in VILLERS-AU-FLOS	MCH
-"-	2/9/18		Carried on reconnaissance from south omits at RIENCOURT. Started work on cleaning debris from mud at pumping STATION on the BAPAUME/ALBERT ROAD W of RIENCOURT.	MCH
-"-	3/9/18		127 Bde relieved 127 Bde. During an reconnaissance journey in direction of YPRES Bde decided known Hd Qrs VILLERS-AU-FLOS. This Coy was ordered to move also. Transport left Rencourt at 2 p.m. Orders Recd. Rencourt to move from PYS & THILLOY. On arrival at VILLERS-AU-FLOS it was decided to move forward to BAPAUME when Coy Hd. was established at the HOSPITAL. No 3 Section reported to St Rames & as look for "Booby traps" in dugouts in order of 127 Bde. This Section were diverted to BUS.	MCH
BARASTRE	4/9/18		At 10.15 AM orders were received for a Section to report to St Rames this to go forward with Bde. Work for Booby traps to No 1 Section was detailed moved to BUS at 3.30 AM. This Section made later in the day to YPRES Reps No 3 & 4 Section standing by ready known at short notice. At 7.30 pm No 3 Section reported forward to St Rames thro' _____ during very little work. From 6am to 8.30 pm succeeding gen were provided in camp.	MCH
-"-	5/9/18		Moved in H.M. to point at BARASTRE. No 1 Section still work at St. Rames the men working from various K of YPRES were very different owing to enemy shelling - friendly with made on turn on CHALK 600 yds E. of YPRES were examined & found in good condition appeared for these mines. Orders received at 12MID to be prepared at short with 2 NZ Div. Coy do own run was being relieved by NZ Div AT 12.30 PM orders received at Coy Hd would more to E. PYS - this was cancelled and very was ordered to PYS. AT 4 p.m. further orders was received and try was ordered to move into area between 2nd NZ Field & to PYS. THILLOY, Y.W. VILLERS. THILLOY, & PYS. & move on to L of PYS. this was to be reached at 10 p.m. by water party to PYS First was to be received & PYS area while working. Halted	MCH

WAR DIARY
INTELLIGENCE SUMMARY
(Erase heading not required.)

Army Form C. 2118.

SHEET 57c

Place	Date	Hour	Summary of Events and Information	Remarks and references to Appendices
PYS	6/9/18		Coy arrived by motor lorry in daylight much from BAPAISTRE. Lorries proceeding from Coy. Lorries drew up with MGR with and the No.1 Section reporting from Coy Lorries drew up with little MGR mess and Rat Hours on PAIX on Road Route. Staff. Short day in waking went comfortable & started work on Rat Hours for 15d groups - curtailed prior for PAIX on Road. Met M2 & S-9	MOH
—	7/9/18		Carried in improving camp - Completed Rat Hours. Carried TURNER Jones Reprieved Cov from lines in U.K.	MOH
—	8/9/18		hand of Coy as bed. did running valid jobs Towards Company Comfortable.	MOH
—	9/9/18		As on 8d	MOH
—	10/9/18		Started morning training - under Section suprvisrs in 12th Sig Adv. in P13 & 15 F. Clear order drill - Rifle drill - Lewis gun & Vickers class 9 M Grd & a few Sapphire in bayonetting - Field Marching. Driven thoroughly tested P10 & 13F in musketry. Orders were drawn to Gourms.	MOH
—	11/9/18		As on 10d	MOH
—	12/9/18		— do —	MOH
—	13/9/18		— do — Corpl: handed N/D M N°44312/Sapper FINLAY, T.H. at BM 11 & 12/7/18 awarded 90 days F.P. N°1	MOH
—	14/9/18		LT HUGHES returned from leave in UK superally at CRE to await army demny order from CRE	MOH
—	15/9/18		— do —	MOH
—	16/9/18		Recruiting Competition Practice - Sent N°2 Sect to FREMICOURT in order from CRE Company Competition	MOH
—	17/9/18		— do —	MOH
—	18/9/18		Training as on 10d Mar Medium Company & GRÉVILLERS & not under CRE 4th Corps Troops	MOH
—	19/9/18		Training on 10d - Major MAYNER and CAPT JONES met 2 MGR mid. K ALBUQUERE K in road to and by 15th Field Coy 37 DN met 2 view to faking over in relief	MOH
—	20/9/18		Training and Coy Route March	MOH
—	21/9/18		Training as above - LT HUGHES attached K 416th Field Coy in order from CRE.	MOH

Army Form C.2118.

WAR DIARY
INTELLIGENCE SUMMARY.
(Erase heading not required.)

SHEET 57C.

Instructions regarding War Diaries and Intelligence Summaries are contained in F.S. Regs., Part II. and the Staff Manual respectively. Title pages will be prepared in manuscript.

Place	Date	Hour	Summary of Events and Information	Remarks and references to Appendices
PYS	2/9/18		No 2 Section received back. Sent men & Tools men R.E. dumps and ration supplies in new A.V. Area around FREMICOURT - BEUGNY - LEBUCQUIERE - VELU	MCH
PYS and LEBUCQUIERE	22/9/18		Left camp by hard walk at 7.30 A.M. passing forest at 8 P.M. arriving at new camp at 11.30 A.M. at LEBUCQUIERE (57c NW I28.65.1). Such afternoon spent reconnoitering new water supply & repairing & running pumps for occupation of infantry and other units - worked on Boulle Red Su, Hd.	MCH
LEBUCQUIERE	23/9/18		Work on stated alm - from 8 A.M. to 5 P.M. - No 3 Sub Section KNOWLTH recommended slightly in leg by shell fire near CRAYTONS CROSS - BEVIS KNOWLTH Hd wounded while working nr. HARINCOURT WOOD	MCH
- do -	24/9/18		En re a-do- FOUR men absent	MCH
- do -	25/9/18		- do -	MCH
- do -	26/9/18		- do - At 3 A.M. received orders that No. IV Sub Sec to attack by 12th and Amending Brigades supporting the attack towards the and both S.L.F. 7 & I.F. left of 12th attacked at 7.30 a.m. men available for laying the battery tapes in dugouts and horses a fin Hd sub. No. Putting up two camouflaged screens for spec. dawn - 10 p.m. receiving tins for spec. column	MCH
		9.20 A.M 23rd Suppt. - 5.20 A.M. 27th Suppt. - Any others by the men	
- do -	27/9/18		Ambulance equipment f/s three lorry was loaned up at dump artillery and used by orders f. C.R.E. & BERTINCOURT driven in and placed on the line and renew two guns at BERTINCOURT equipments is BERTINCOURT on my incl. Hd and Hd sheldon ammunition lorry was ordered from K1.26 I Suff/Sd. at K 36a 5.3 to reinj. of the new sandbag employed from stall He Any was being utilised by No 2 Sub in light refin field. Cart wounded and am. wounded...	MCH
BERTINCOURT	29/9/18		BERTINCOURT demolishing to Hd P/K S.I - Work in ad. ponds Rode at IS-10 - ROUTMERCOURT. and METZ	MCH
- do -	30/9/18		Horse on time - arranged with W O. Hd Ealing of was for lay trained Am in to run - marking the men given the equipment returned nil to mn.	MCH

M. McCormick Major, R.E.
O.C. 429th Fd. Coy. R.E.

Army Form C. 2118.

Vol 21

WAR DIARY
or
INTELLIGENCE SUMMARY.
(Erase heading not required.)

429th Field Coy. R.E.

October 1918

Volume 4

WAR DIARY or INTELLIGENCE SUMMARY

Army Form C. 2118.

Instructions regarding War Diaries and Intelligence Summaries are contained in F.S. Regs., Part II. and the Staff Manual respectively. Title pages will be prepared in manuscript.

(Erase heading not required)

SHEETS 57 & 57B.

Place	Date	Hour	Summary of Events and Information	Remarks and references to Appendices
BERTINCOURT	1/10/18		OC and Capt Ross went out & reconnoitred bridges over ESCAULT CANAL at MARCOING and NURLU MEREL. No 1 and 3 SECTIONS moved to neighbourhood of TRESCAULT for work in new No H.L. Sectn	men
TRESCAULT	2/10/18		Reconnaissance of area & work in neighbourhood of TRESCAULT at K36.c.1.6. No 1 Section moved to Q10 central & the new site at No H.L.	men
do	3/10/18		Worked on new site at Q10 central – Section Mess Bivouacs being erected.	men
do	4/10/18		Moved HQ and No 3 Sect to TRESCAULT/RIDGECOURT Road – Reception Camp in old G.R.E.	men cept
do	5/10/18		Work as above. Transport Lines moved up & HQ in BERTINCOURT MARRINCOURT Road	men
do	6/10/18		do	men
do	7/10/18		do	men
do	8/10/18		do. No 2 Section moved to BERTINCOURT RUYAULCOURT Rd	men
do	9/10/18		do. No 2 Section rejoined Company	men
LESDAINS	10/10/18		Company moved to LESDAINS and Karee Park – No 3 Section remains behind and – 2nd parts to BETHE ESNES & later for booby traps –	men
do	11/10/18		Have looked after pump work & dry walks	men
do	12/10/18		Section being used loading bombs for Bridge over ESCAULT CANAL for war over river SELLE near BRIASTRE	men
BEAUVOIS	13/10/18		Company moved about to BEAUVOIS expt Section – looking work on road	men
do	14/10/18		Company worked on road cratered with 1/7 Bn NF	men
do	15/10/18		do	men
do	16/10/18		do	men

Army Form C. 2118.

WAR DIARY
or
INTELLIGENCE SUMMARY.
(Erase heading not required.)

Instructions regarding War Diaries and Intelligence Summaries are contained in F. S. Regs., Part II. and the Staff Manual respectively. Title pages will be prepared in manuscript.

SHEETS 57?

Place	Date	Hour	Summary of Events and Information	Remarks and references to Appendices
BEAUVOIS	17-10-18		Company working on shelters for Bde Road Hd.	MR1
-//-	18.10.18		- do - also tunnelled dug-outs for Batt Road Hd.	MR1
-//-	19.10.18		- do - Twelve reached from advance at TRONCHIENS for holding positions	MR1
-//-	20.10.18		Anxious resumed the advance about 1030 - died 2Lt D.C. CHAPMAN 2/6 wes killed at 0630 and 19.10.73. 2nd Cpl. COLLINS.W and MURRAY SAPPER LATHAM were wounded by shell nr BRIASTRE. Sent Lieut J.F.N. MEDDISON party on road BRIASTRE/SOLESMES and MUURET/SUPPER LATHAM were wounded by shell. 2 Lt JFN MEDDISON Scored 4 SOLESMES down up old demolition taken for Repair - Scouts used bij demolition taken for Repair -	MR1
-//-	21.10.18		Buried 2Lt D.C. CHAPMAN at BEAUVOIS CIVILIAN cemetery - Company removed mines in demolition 4 roadway bridge ouver the Sheet - Put up Bde Road Hd at BELLE VUE - Bunted litter dispatch on BEAUVOIS/MESSY TREAT. Work on Bridge nr COVINS n shill fair-	MR1
-//-	22.10.18		Demolition 4 bridge was carried on. A 17ft Fosffre way being cleared before evening - work carried on returning round preventing these tra.-	MR1
-//-	23.10.18		Work on road m BEAUVOIS/MESSY continued - M2 division going through. Work resumed the advance at 0300. Bridge at E7c7.3 was carried on. Heavy Traffic caused some interruption. Lieut PAUL R.E went forward alone to reconnoitre Bridges over BEARD BROOK East of SOLESMES found him in good condition	☆☆
SOLESMES	24.10.18		Demolition of bridge at E7c7.3 was completed. Company moved forward into SOLESMES. Treated in billets with decorations Ed. E7c.9.7 and four bins at E7c.9.9 Major M.S. HANNER R.E. Eft for Leau to U.K. Order received to refair a junction Bridge at TRIASTRE by a	☆☆
	25.10.18		Cleaning up to-do - Order recd to refair a junction Bridge at TRIASTRE by a Knoff left bridge	☆☆
	26.10.18		Tins to collected to a days prepared by Lieut H.L. POOL for truck bridge at BRIASTRE. Remainig available	☆☆
	27.10.18		new of the employ Reynolds in employees in availing any transport here. QM stores et. transfer into SOLESMES. 2 other offices	☆☆

Army Form C. 2118.

WAR DIARY
or
INTELLIGENCE SUMMARY.
(Erase heading not required.)

Instructions regarding War Diaries and Intelligence Summaries are contained in F.S. Regs., Part II. and the Staff Manual respectively. Title pages will be prepared in manuscript.

Place	Date	Hour	Summary of Events and Information	Remarks and references to Appendices
SOLESMES	28.10.18		2 section bridging & training.	CRE
	29.10.18		Ditto.	CRE
	30.10.18		Ditto. 2/Lieut. F.W. STAPLETON reported from Base as reinforcement. 2/Lieut. D. STEVENSON joined company. Transfers from 427 Fd.S.C. R.E., to fill vacancy caused by Lieut. J.V. HUGHES appoints 2nd in command 427 Fd.S & R.E. with acting rank of captain.	CRE
	31.10.18		One section bridging. Coy. Hqrs. now preparing to divisional H.E. sports, as transport show, to be held at TRAIELLE R.V. 9. Nov.	CRE

[signature]
Capt R.E.
O.C. 422th Fd. Coy. R.E.

429 Fd Cdt A RE
Army Form C. 2118.

Vol 27

WAR DIARY
or
INTELLIGENCE SUMMARY.
(Erase heading not required.)

WAR DIARY

NOVEMBER 1918.

VOLUME 4.

429th FIELD COY RE

Army Form C. 2118.

WAR DIARY
INTELLIGENCE SUMMARY.
(Erase heading not required.)

Instructions regarding War Diaries and Intelligence Summaries are contained in F.S. Regs. Part II. and the Staff Manual respectively. Title pages will be prepared in manuscript.

Place	Date	Hour	Summary of Events and Information	Remarks and references to Appendices
SOLESMES	1-11-18		12 Div & R.E. Spoke to Transport Competition Ltd at PRAYELLE near VIESLY.	CBff
—	2-11-18		1 motor cyclist, small details on route bridge at BRIASTRE. Remainder training.	CBff
—	3-11-18		1 motor running fanton from BRIASTRE and thing near formed to N.Z. dump at SOLESMES.	CBff
—	4-11-18		Advance resumed by N.Z. Div. 2/Lt D. STEVENSON attached to 4th C.R.E. as forward company with a view to taking over from Div. any bridge which night be encountered during the advance.	CBff
LE QUESNOY	5-11-18		Company moved to LE QUESNOY. No action. No bridges to repair. Leave for 12 Div. Div H.Q. known moved on to POTELLE. No action required at LE QUESNOY in the evening.	CBff
LE CARNOY	6-11-18		No 1 motor moved to POTELLE CHATEAU. Lovely trip during the morning. The company moved to LE CARNOY arriving early afternoon. No 3 motor sent early afternoon to form a ponton dump at PONT BILLON near POTELLE. Fallen wagons also met there.	
		1515	Sheet 51 M 28 & 2.8 N 31 a 2.9	
		1600	Orders to take over from N.Z. Div. Helker trestles & superstructure at 1600 hrs at MAISON ROUGE Sheet 51 N 31 a 2.9 and bridge a crater in MORMAL FOREST in N 35. Took transport taken over and all available men out. Late found that it was expected that all work and labour to be carried out ½ mile. Late found this material end to gather the work by transport and as rifle was not kn ofc unloading, being nature 2 and 4 etc complete job. Crater bridge completed.	CBff
LE CARNOY PRENT BAIRY	7-11-18	2300	Orders to move at 1400 hrs to the BAVAI - PONTSUR- SAMBRE Road in Q 22, Q 28, Q 34 Move. Difficulties in MORMAL FOREST owing to craters, road diversion at FORESTER'S HOUSE N 36 a not being out etc.	CBff
		1100	Diamonds to Sapper Company arrived in billets in Q 29.	
		1400	No 3 motor also moved up forward in to position.	
		2200	Transport arrived in new billets O25. Approx 2000 Germ ponton party arrived.	
	8-11-18	0030	Teams and loading parts sent back for more pontons.	
		0300	No 4 motor out to BOUSSIERES arrived with Major R.SOMBRE.	
		0500	Heller trestle out to repair damaged road bridge at O 30 d 8.2. Reconnaissance party also out to inspect	
		0630	road & BOUSSIERES. No 1 motor met at fragile bridge at O 30 d 8.2 which Lieut Pirch set out road	
		0800	diversion to bypass frank bridge. A & B BOUSSIERES P 32 Q 2.9.	
			No 3 motor at towing pontons went up to BOUSSIERES and bridge was put across during the afternoon. Late orders	
		1100	1/2 N.F. (?) went up along to BOUSSIERES and No 2 motor was sent up 6 pm No 3. Lieut FISHER, 0 2/Lt. STEVENSON	CBff

WAR DIARY

INTELLIGENCE SUMMARY

(Erase heading not required.)

Army Form C. 2118.

Instructions regarding War Diaries and Intelligence Summaries are contained in F.S. Regs., Part II. and the Staff Manual respectively. Title pages will be prepared in manuscript.

Place	Date	Hour	Summary of Events and Information	Remarks and references to Appendices
PETIT BAYAI & BOUSSIERES	9-11-18		Road diversion at P.32.d.29 was carried on from 0700 to 1700 army 2 section R.E., 1 company N.F. (?) and a continuous fatty of 1 company infantry — also one German prisoner. Continued from 0900 during the afternoon. Lt. Col. Stevenson returned from 427 Fd. Coy and went to join No 2 section at Boussières. Various road mines were marked and removed during the day.	CBJ
LOUVROIL	10-11-18		Sections 2 and 3 went early to HAUTMONT to assist in constructing Infantry Bridge. Company moved to LOUVROIL. Shot 5, Q.20.a and b. Section 2 & 3 rejoined then with in afternoon and section 3 & 4 then moved on to FERRIERE-LA-GRANDE to work on a bridge at Q.23.a.9.0 over R. SOLRE.	CBJ
LOUVROIL & FERRIERE	11-11-18	0700	Work commenced on trestle bridge at Q.23.a.9.0 working 2 shifts — no section on each shift and 30 Infantry & 1 N. Coy N.F. on each shift. Paty of 12 No 2 section went to FERRIERE-LA-PETITE by get to work on 2 bdys at Q.36.c.70.25 and Q.36.c.95.25. Grenades came to force and hostilities were suspended.	CBJ
" "	12-11-18	1100	Work continued on bridge at FERRIERE-LA-GRANDE and FERRIERE-LA-PETITE. Paty of No 2 section working at FERRIERE-LA-PETITE went to Bin at FERRIERE-LA-GRANDE with section 3 and 4. Hose lines moved into HAUTMONT and arrangements were made to billet the whole company in HAUTMONT during this day.	CBJ
		1330	On arr. on work on bridges arr finished. FERRIERE-LA-PETITE bridge was finished this day. No 2 section and parties of Coy HQ, No 1 section and parties of No 2 section moved into HAUTMONT. Work on bridge at FERRIERE-LA-GRANDE continued.	CBJ
LOUVROIL, FERRIERE, HAUTMONT	13-11-18		Bridge at Q.23.a.9.0 completed and handed to long traffic about noon. Orders were received during the morning to take over bridge at Q.17.c.6.2 from 62 Div. Fmng Pty and 3 fd companies working under the sheds on it. Arrange to take over at 0800 hrs on 15-11-18.	CBJ
HAUTMONT & FERRIERE	14-11-18		Major M.S. HANMER R.E. returned from leave. Bridge at Q.17.c.8.2 taken over. Trestle and R.S.J. roadbearers already in position. Toolen for decking from S. a factory at Q.17 central and this was used. The bridge was completed for traffic by evening but orders were then received to make it fit for N. loads. This involved strengthening the trestles.	CBJ
" "	15-11-18	0800		CBJ
" "	16-11-18		Extra beys added trestles in bridge at Q.17.c.8.2. Completed for N. loads by evening. Work at HAUTMONT in hand was army in fi. infantry & foam billets, approvement of own company billets and cleaning up of transport.	CBJ

WAR DIARY
INTELLIGENCE SUMMARY
(Erase heading not required.)

Army Form C. 2118.

Instructions regarding War Diaries and Intelligence Summaries are contained in F. S. Regs., Part II. and the Staff Manual respectively. Title pages will be prepared in manuscript.

Place	Date	Hour	Summary of Events and Information	Remarks and references to Appendices
HAUTMONT	17-11-18		Party from FERRIERE came to HAUTMONT. Being maintained party of 1 NCO and 5 sappers to watch bridges till night of 18/19 Nov.	
—	18-11-18		System appts B Lewis. 1 section to work on improvement of billets. 1 on improvement of Infantry billets. 1 on transport lines ad 1 resting. Demobilization scheme explained as appears taken to investigate possibility of starting a Divl Tr[?] Sch. Company recreation room started.	
—	19-11-18			
—	20-11-18			
—	21-11-18		Work as above	
—	22-11-18		do	
—	23-11-18		Two sections employed in ascertaining [?] Rds to RE in Army bridges at LOUVROIL — 1 section working as on work lines	
—	24-11-18		One section employed on bridges at LOUVROIL — one section + one testing + one on work lines	
—	25-11-18		Work as above	
—	26-11-18			
—	27-11-18			
—	28-11-18		Work as above	
—	29-11-18			
—	30-11-18		Instructions received information that N° 457 Army Tp H.M.R.E.R. S.M. had died of [?] Lues use at N° 4 C.C.S.	

M.O. [signature]
Major RE
O.C. 72nd [?]

Army Form C. 2118.

WAR DIARY
or
INTELLIGENCE SUMMARY.
(Erase heading not required.)

429th FIELD COY R.E.

DECEMBER 1918.

VOLUME 4

WAR DIARY
INTELLIGENCE SUMMARY.
(Erase heading not required.)

Army Form C. 2118.

Instructions regarding War Diaries and Intelligence Summaries are contained in F.S. Regs., Part II. and the Staff Manual respectively. Title pages will be prepared in manuscript.

Place	Date	Hour	Summary of Events and Information	Remarks and references to Appendices
HAUTMONT	1-12-18 to 5-12-18		Work in hand :- Improvements to sanitary billets, painting vehicles, one section for day meetings, occasional small jobs to L.S.F. infantry & improve billets	CPJ
	6-12-18		Major M.S. HANMER with No 1 section and one section from each of the two other sections and a platoon of pioneers left HAUTMONT en route for CHARLEROI to prepare for the division to meet the CHARLEROI Area. Move of the division contemplated about 14th inst. This Advance Party moved in 3 stages. 1st day to BINCHE 2nd day to FONTAINE L'EVEQUE 3rd day to CHARLEROI.	CPJ
			Section 2,3,4 with section transport moved under Lieut. H.J. PAUL to VIEUX RENG to work a bridge. Transport lines and HQ remained at HAUTMONT.	
HAUTMONT, VIEUX RENG and CHARLEROI	7-12-18		Sections 2,3,4 started work on bridges and culvert.	CPJ
	8-12-18		Advance party arrived CHARLEROI at noon.	CPJ
	9-12-18		Advance party started work on billets, improvements, chimneys, latrines etc.	CPJ
	10-12-18		Advance party continued same work and also started work on billets for 125 Inf Bde. The party at VIEUX RENG completed the bridge which was opened to traffic in the evening.	CPJ
	11-12-18		Advance party on 8-10th and VIEUX RENG party worked on approach road to bridge and prepared to move the next day.	CPJ
	12-12-18		Sections 2,3,4 moved by lorry to CHARLEROI and joined the advance party. Section transport & these 3 sections marched to BINCHE.	CPJ
	13-12-18		Transport & section 2,3,4 moved from BINCHE to CHARLEROI.	CPJ
	14-12-18		Section transport from HAUTMONT started to move to CHARLEROI. Marched with 127 Inf Bde to BOUSSOIS	CPJ
	15-12-18		Transport moved from BOUSSOIS to PEISSANT. Remainder of company at CHARLEROI continued to work on billets etc.	CPJ

Army Form C. 2118.

WAR DIARY
INTELLIGENCE SUMMARY.
(Erase heading not required.)

Instructions regarding War Diaries and Intelligence Summaries are contained in F.S. Regs., Part II. and the Staff Manual respectively. Title pages will be prepared in manuscript.

Place	Date	Hour	Summary of Events and Information	Remarks and references to Appendices
CHARLEROI	16/12/18		Transport moved from TEISSANT to LEVAL TRAHEGUIES. Company at CHARLEROI continued work in preparation of billets.	Copy
	17/12/18		Transport rested at LEVAL TRAHEGUIES.	Copy
	18/12/18		Transport completed the march to CHARLEROI	Copy
	19-12-18		Work was continued on infantry billets, baths, etc. 'A' Brigade workshop was	Copy
	21-12-18		started for 125 Inf Bde, also the infantry barracks, for supply of tables, latrine seats etc.	Copy
	22-12-18		Resting.	Copy
	23-12-18		Continued work on billets up to 12.30 pm on 24th inst. Dvr WILLIAMS left for demobilization on	Copy
	24-12-18			Copy
	25-12-18		No work. S/Sgt OSBORNE left for demobilization on 26th inst.	Copy
	26-12-18			Copy
	27-12-18		Work continued up to 12.30 pm on 28th inst.	Copy
	28-12-18			Copy
	29-12-18		Resting	Copy
	30-12-18		Work continued on billets. Fourth Army Regulating Staging Camp at JUMET. Beds etc to be installed.	Copy
	31-12-18		Work started on a	Copy

M. Hannum
Major, R.E.
O.C. 429th Fd. Coy. R.E.

429TH FIELD COMPANY, R.E.

WAR DIARY
or
INTELLIGENCE SUMMARY.

Army Form C. 2118.

4/29 Fld Coy R.E.

(Erase heading not required)

Place	Date	Hour	Summary of Events and Information	Remarks and references to Appendices
CHARLEROI	1/1/19		Two Lectures morning under Lieut. H.I. Peak at JUMET - other stations returns at Cavalry Infantry Camp at Ariendroutier and Company lines - Divisional Ronds - Work as above	MEN
-//-	2/1/19		- do -	MEN
-//-	3/1/19		- do -	MEN
-//-	4/1/19		- do -	MEN
-//-	5/1/19		No work - Church Parade in morning	MEN
-//-	6/1/19		work as on 4th	MEN
-//-	7/1/19		- do -	MEN
-//-	8/1/19		- do -	MEN
-//-	9/1/19		- do - The following men were ordered for demobilization: No 18008 Cpl Toriguton F.A. No 442647 2nd Cpl Morris H.B. No 161 2/c Sergt S No 164323 Sapper Gunter F. No 442585 Sapper Hopkins J. No 620/3 Sapper Lomant H. No 21745 Sapper Rook A. No 478591 Sapper Spooner R.	MEN
-//-	10/1/19		Work in JUMET Camp as described. Carried on work. The following Sappers and NCO were in and after work. The work during afternoon were released for demobilization. Lieut. Nicolson J & Hargreaves G W.S. Walker R.	MEN
-//-	11/1/19		Carried on work as on 9th. Returning men were released for demobilization. No 443362 Lc Cpl Wheat A. No 448257 Sapper Marsden H No 442321 2/c Warren H	MEN
-//-	12/1/19		No work in afternoon	MEN
-//-	13/1/19		No work. Church Parade in morning.	MEN
-//-	14/1/19		work on as on 11th	MEN
-//-	15/1/19		- do - The following NCOs and men were released for demobilization. No .... Sergt Harris S. No 33..... 2nd Cpl Spencer W. No 442073 2/c Parrish S No 27780 2/c Needham A.S. No56604 Sapper Stronge W. No 449905 Sapper Pavy Le C.	MEN

WAR DIARY
or
INTELLIGENCE SUMMARY.
(Erase heading not required.)

Army Form C. 2118.

Place	Date	Hour	Summary of Events and Information	Remarks and references to Appendices
CHARLEROI	15-1-19		Works as on 14th. Half day H	MOH
"	16-1-19		do	MOH
"	17-1-19		do	MOH
"	18-1-19		do. Half day H. The following men were sent for demobilisation: No 440053 Sapper Ryalmore HF, No 442216 - Sues G.T, No 516190 - Trenfy G.H, 480457 - Finch G, 488811	MOH
"	19-1-19		Rest. Church parade ordr -	MOH
"	20-1-19		Work as above. No 166805 Sapper Ainsley S. due to leave	MOH
"	21-1-19		do. The following men sent for demobilisation No 477036 2/L Jamieson W, No 304310	MOH
"			2/C Martin H. No 447187 Sapper Sigrist T, No 341993 Sapper Archive G, No 428700 Sapper	MOH
"			Ford B, No 495094 2/C Poland S, No 514863 Sapper Avery F.G, No 300706 Sapper Cowdace E	
"	23-1-19		Work as above. Half day H. No 400026 Sapper Watson A, No 495395 Sapper Gripper A.H.	MOH
"			demobilized	
"	23-1-19		Work as above. C.R.E. inspected Billets & prior to divisional ammunition inspection	MOH
"	24-1-19		do C.R.E. inspected horse lines -	MOH
"	25-1-19		do Half day H	MOH
"	26-1-19		Rest. Church Parade. The following men sent for demobilisation No 447267 Cpl Caden P.G, No 447339	MOH
			Sapper Wood H. No 447380 Sapper White W. No 447470 Sapper Peacock G, No 312152 Sapper Murray T	MOH
			No 36407 Pioneer G McBain, Driver A, No 465735 Sapper Bingen T, No 235990 Sapper Gillen C, No 108679 Pnr Milne A.M	MOH

WAR DIARY
or
INTELLIGENCE SUMMARY.
(Erase heading not required.)

Army Form C. 2118.

Place	Date	Hour	Summary of Events and Information	Remarks and references to Appendices
NAPLES	27.1.19		NAPLES - A few men in bed sonerries. Repair work at REDOUBT. Parties inspected bridges nr. Benito in town and it was alleged that the Frenchmen had left a barge of unserbly? appliances in bridge which are attd needs. Airstream were formed. M⁰ 486090 sapper Reader L.H. & M⁰ 473261 sapper Daniels A. dismstrsigned.	MOH
"	28.1.19		Work in Barracks the usual. Armoured car woods inspected. Rations distributed.	MOH
"	29.1.19		Work as above - kit exam M/- following cut for dismstrsigned 17.4.1.170 sapper Nightingale N⁰ 410519 sapper Crawford N M⁰ 471173 Cpl Kersden T.M. M⁰ 4440677 Y Cpl Band M⁰ 468144 sapper Lipsey E. M⁰ 30494 sapper Ricely T. M⁰ acts & 3× screen mellon N. M⁰ 28068 sapper broadbent a. M⁰ 425356 sapper Boteford"	MOH
"	30.1.19		troops as above	MOH
"	31.1.19		troops as above	MOH

W.R. Herman Major
Comdg 429 Fld Co RE

Army Form C. 2118

WAR DIARY
~~INTELLIGENCE SUMMARY~~
(Erase heading not required.)

WO 95 2125

429th FIELD Coy R.E.

February 1919.

Volume 5

WAR DIARY
INTELLIGENCE SUMMARY.

Army Form C. 2118.

(Erase heading not required.)

Instructions regarding War Diaries and Intelligence Summaries are contained in F. S. Regs., Part II. and the Staff Manual respectively. Title pages will be prepared in manuscript.

Place	Date	Hour	Summary of Events and Information	Remarks and references to Appendices
CHARLEROI	1/2/19		25 P.O.W. reported to work in the 3 Companies have been used in loads put on hand billage Equipmt. Min. Repairs Kitchens, midden & latrines - Missing MONTIGNY - Rue Kerk app Sgt Ainsles	MGH
-/-	2.2.19		Rest	MGH
-/-	3.2.19		Working party mining unused P.O.W. Shed anowday 4thBry at Ron Shuts	MGH
			The following were demobilized No 440876 Sapper GIBB R. No 5447 Sapper RONIE No 198744 Sapper DAVIS J. T. No 440909 Sapper BERRY F.C. No 495317 Capper CARVER S. No 21454 MAW H. No 241953 Sapper PHILLIPS. No 440163 YOUNG F.E.M. No 211910 Sapper ENSWORTH T. No 440276 Sapper COOPER J. No 443837 Sapper SUTCLIFFE H No 38099 At DENNETERE NOUVEAU Lt JONESS No 15 2505 At MILTON H. No 448771 MONCKTON W.	
-/-	4.2.19		Rest & Church no 3rd	MGH
-/-	5.2.19		- do -	MGH
-/-	6.2.19		- do - The following men have been demobilized No 16539 Cpl OLIVER A. AD PASMIMAGEE POST	Both MGH
-/-	7.2.19		- do -	
-/-	8.2.19		- do - Working party CORNERS & NOUVELLES	MGH
			Cpl SMITH T.V. No 443.161 Sapper LEVER A. No 104075 Sapper TUCK A No 432209 At JONESS	
-/-	9.2.19		No 144 190 Cpl GARRATY R No 87 46 At JAMESSON F. RMH	MGH
-/-	10.2.19		Men have been repairing spending mains - will do repair both din	MGH
	11.2.19			
	12.2.19		Most as abre. The following men were held for demobilization No 443474 Cpl KERRIS	MGH
	13.2.20		No 443 368 Sapper SOOTH MOUSING Sapper CORLING H.A. No 46559 Sapper HUDSON T. MONSERN At GARDNER T.	MGH

Army Form C. 2118.

WAR DIARY
or
INTELLIGENCE SUMMARY.
(Erase heading not required.)

Instructions regarding War Diaries and Intelligence Summaries are contained in F. S. Regs., Part II. and the Staff Manual respectively. Title pages will be prepared in manuscript.

Place	Date	Hour	Summary of Events and Information	Remarks and references to Appendices
CHARLEROI	14.2.19		Fit an 13 J	M24
"	15.2.19		do	M24
"	16.2.19		Rest. The following men were sent for demobilisation Nº 40205 CSM Corbett H. Nº 44012 Cpl. BRIGHTMORE R. Nº 443031 Cpl BRAKEWELL R. Nº 441118 Spr Hodge H. Nº 44119 Spr SABB. G. Nº 39610 Spr RUTTER R. Nº 146470 St Mne G.	M24
"	17.2.19		Arranged to supply Staff Supra Sub Yard, and 2 lines. The wire being carried out by 1st Pioneers Bn A.I.F. Started erecting 3 lines for demobilisation.	M24
"	18.2.19		-do-	M24
"	19.2.19		-do- A Pile horse cast at stable at about 17.30 - all available men cut from dy. killed. Own before arrival Veterinary Surgeon. Pile was shot about 18.00 - The following men were sent for demobilisation Nº 369290 Sp Peterson E.	M24
"	20.2.19		Fire as above. Started training in demolition. Charges of TNT.	M24
"	21.2.19		-do- find training in demolition Nº 44010 Sergt EVANS M.P. Nº 440012 Sergt EMERY N. Nº 141501 Spr PENNINGTON T.S. Nº 470459 Spr SMAILS A. Nº 50406 Spr COOPER H.W. Nº 50062 Spr WILSON W.E. Nº 31104 Spr AVERY M.	M24
"	22.2.19		Wire as above - Fire training for demolition. Nº 49679 Sapr MAYNARD F.T. Nº 441075 Sapr COLES.S. Nº 441165 Sapr BENNETT J. Nº 199990 Sapr NORMAN. M. Nº 40583 Sapr BOWMAN W.	M24
"	23.2.19		Rest	M24
"	24.2.19 25.2.19		Stores carapax taken to Parade ground in readiness. Individual cheches. Ammunition stores put in one side for inspection 9 am. 26.2.19 The following men were demobilised during the week in turn in UK. Nº 12973 Spr Johnson H. Nº 4731 Spr Munson W. Nº 13438 Sapr Frosty & Nº 43805 St. Gilling J.	M24

M. Steverburgh
Mnjr Cmdg 176 TRE

WAR DIARY
INTELLIGENCE SUMMARY

(Erase heading not required.)

Army Form C. 2118.

42 Div 26

429th FIELD Co. R.E.

MARCH 1919

Volume 5

WAR DIARY
INTELLIGENCE SUMMARY

Army Form C. 2118

Place	Date	Hour	Summary of Events and Information	Remarks and references to Appendices
CHARLEROI BELGIUM	1.3.19 to 19.3.19		Coy. no. working checking & packing stores for demobilization and overhauling walls & sale of plant & salvage thereof by public auction & transportation	
	2.3.19		Capt C.E.T. JONES left to take over command of 210th Field Coy RE	
	5.3.19		Lieut. GOODWIN & Spr. HOLLETTS left for disposal	
	6.3.19		Spr. WILLIAMS G, Rfmn PERCIVAL & PETTENER, Driv H. THOMPSON & Spr TOMLIN T.H. SHERRIFF & DON appointment Major M.S. HANMER left for U.K. for demobilization. 2nd Lt J. PAUL took over Command of Company	A.M.
	19.3.19		Spr. A.E. JOHNSON & Driver L.S. BEHAR left for disposal	
	22.3.19		Corpl T. CRAIG & 15 O.R. left for 1st Div. – to report to CRE 1st Div	
	15.3.19		2/Cpl A. COOPER, Spr T.E. WRIGHT left for 3rd Div who have been sent (reinforced). Driver STURDEY left for disposal	
	29.3.19		Entire entrained at Charleroi to proceed to U.K. Lt. STEVENSON kangarts 4/97 C	

JPaul, Lt.
O.C. (acting) 429 Field Coy R.E.

www.ingramcontent.com/pod-product-compliance
Lightning Source LLC
Chambersburg PA
CBHW081538160426
43191CB00011B/1788